Vinyl Theory

Jeffrey R. Di Leo

LEVER
PRESS

The complete manuscript of this work was subjected to a partly closed ("single blind") review process. For more information, please see our Peer Review Commitments and Guidelines at https://www.leverpress.org/peerreview

DOI: https://doi.org/10.3998/mpub.11676127
Print ISBN: 978-1-64315-015-4
Open access ISBN: 978-1-64315-016-1

Library of Congress Control Number: 2019954611

Published in the United States of America by Lever Press, in partnership with Amherst College Press and Michigan Publishing

Without music, life would be an error.

—Friedrich Nietzsche

The preservation of music in records reminds one of canned food.

—Theodor W. Adorno

Contents

Member Institution Acknowledgments

Lever Press is a joint venture. This work was made possible by the generous support of Lever Press member libraries from the following institutions:

Adrian College

Agnes Scott College

Allegheny College

Amherst College

Bard College

Berea College

Bowdoin College

Carleton College

Claremont Graduate
    University

Claremont McKenna College

Clark Atlanta University

Coe College

College of Saint Benedict /
    Saint John's University

The College of Wooster

Denison University

DePauw University

Earlham College

Furman University

Grinnell College

Hamilton College

Harvey Mudd College

Haverford College

Hollins University

Keck Graduate Institute

Kenyon College

Knox College

Lafayette College Library

Lake Forest College

Macalester College

Middlebury College

Morehouse College
Oberlin College
Pitzer College
Pomona College
Rollins College
Santa Clara University
Scripps College
Sewanee: The University of the
    South
Skidmore College
Smith College
Spelman College
St. Lawrence University

St. Olaf College
Susquehanna University
Swarthmore College
Trinity University
Union College
University of Puget Sound
Ursinus College
Vassar College
Washington and Lee
    University
Whitman College
Willamette University
Williams College

PREFACE

Vinyl Theory is a book about the intersection of vinyl records with critical theory. It is the product of a writer who grew up with vinyl records and holds a deep appreciation for them. It is also the intervention of a scholar deeply committed to expanding the range of thought associated with literary and cultural theory into areas where it has not enjoyed a great deal of speculation. Vinyl theory is one of these areas. It is my hope that it encourages other theorists and vinylists to use it to continue a dialogue about vinyl theory. Below is an overview of the path that brought me to write this book and an outline of the major questions it pursues.

⁂

Vinyl record fever hit me early in life. In junior high, I had a friend whose father owned all of the jukeboxes in town. My friend would let me browse through boxes of "decommissioned" 45 rpm records and buy what I wanted for a nickel each. I played them on my parent's huge stereo record cabinet. On the top side of the cabinet were two sliding pieces of wood. Sliding one to the right revealed a storage area for vinyl records. Sliding one to the left revealed an AM/FM radio set next to a record player upon which you could stack albums or 45s on a spindle that released one after the other for "continuous" playback.

It always makes me a little bit envious to read about musicians who say that their parent's record collection was solely classical or blues or jazz and to learn that they would wear the grooves down repeatedly playing early Hot Five Armstrong or Mozart symphonies. The records in our cabinet were nothing like this, though I too wore down the grooves of all of them. Moreover, to say that my parents had a record "collection" is only true in the minimal sense of the term: there were a dozen or so albums in the cabinet but after the movie soundtracks and children's music—stuff like the soundtracks to the 1967 film *Doctor Dolittle* and the 1969 film *Easy Rider* and children's favorites like *Christmas with the Chipmunks* (1962)—the collection consisted of a handful of albums. Lucky for me each of them was a classic: Bob Dylan's *Greatest Hits* (March 1967), Led Zeppelin's first album (January 1969), Janis Joplin's *Pearl* (January 1971), and two albums by The Beatles, *Rubber Soul* (December 1965) and *Meet the Beatles* (January 1964).

Aside from singing or playing on ukulele or recorder as a class at least a couple of the songs from the Dylan album like "Blowin' in the Wind" and "The Times They Are a-Changin'" in elementary school, there was very little connection between the vinyl in our cabinet and my primary school education. Although we learned as a class to sing and play many protest songs, we never really talked about them either musically or philosophically. It would not be until high school and college that courses in music theory would start to open up the wonders of the vinyl world to me. Still, when it was finally opened, it quickly led me away from the vinyl in our cabinet to the worlds of classical music and jazz as they were widely regarded the proper subject of music theory.

In junior high, some of my friends dressed up in costumes and makeup and put on a KISS "concert" for the school. They took to the stage one Saturday evening in full KISS regalia complete with a huge PA system and flashy guitars and drums and played an entire set of KISS music note for note. I know it might be hard to believe, but they pretty much fooled the whole school into believing that they were actually playing the music as opposed to lip-synching and playing air guitar to the 1975 KISS album *Alive!* In fact, I am sure that some of the kids who went to the concert that night still believe that they sang and played all of those songs—and still don't realize that it was really an amplified record. It was only in high school that the story started to leak among the musicians that this was not a "real" concert. Or was it?

Needless to say, as an aspiring young guitar player, the event made a big impression on me and led to my first album purchase: KISS's 1976 album *Rock and Roll Over*. Along with my stack of decommissioned 45s, this record was added to my parent's stereo cabinet. Later that year, a kind family friend bought me a copy of one of his favorite records, Engelbert Humperdinck's 1976 album *After the Lovin'*. But it was not my cup of tea, so I asked my parents if I could return it to the store and exchange it for an album that I liked. They agreed, and soon I added my second album to the cabinet: *Alice Cooper Goes to Hell*—another "treasure" from 1976. The final addition to my junior high album collection was Steve Miller Band's *Fly Like an Eagle* (1976), which holds up better than the Alice Cooper and KISS albums but nowhere close to the Dylan, Beatles, Zeppelin, and Joplin records already in the cabinet.

In high school, I managed to scrape up enough money for my own stereo, which I kept in my room along with my records. But as luck would have it, just as I came of age as a viable consumer of vinyl records, they gave way to eight-track tapes. And then when I started college, eight-tracks were being eclipsed by cassette tapes. To make material matters of musical reproduction even worse, by the time I graduated from college, compact discs were starting to take root as the best way to listen to music without "noise."[1]

Additionally, I also had some recorded music on reel-to-reel tape. This was mainly because as a guitar player, I enjoyed messing around with "Frippertronics," that is, the technique developed by the guitarist Robert Fripp wherein two reel-to-reel tape players are connected together allowing one to overdub multiple guitar parts live to create a sort of symphony (or, if you will, a cacophony) of sounds. At the time, reel-to-reel recorded music was considered by many as the most authentic and best sounding source of recorded music.

As the years passed, vinyl records started to become regarded as an antiquated means of listening to music. Folks started to liquidate their record collections in favor of compact discs, and when downloadable MP3 music became commonplace, compact discs started to go the way of eight-track tapes and vinyl. Not only did record stores, new and used, become more rare,[2] so too did stores that sold compact discs. When Tower Records filed for bankruptcy and liquidation in 2006, and this franchise of record stores established in 1960 shuttered their doors for good, the era of vinyl records appeared to have come to a close.[3]

Nevertheless, the changes in the music industry were not done in a vacuum. Similar changes were also occurring in the book industry. Namely, brick-and-mortar bookstores were closing, and there was a wave of digital book euphoria that commenced in 2007, when Amazon first introduced their Kindle reader. By the time Borders Books closed their four hundred remaining stores in 2011, the bookstore appeared to be going the route of the record store—and the era of digital reading and listening was officially in full swing.

But something strange happened along the way. Not only are printed books and brick-and-mortar bookstores enjoying a renaissance of late, so too are vinyl records. According to a 2017 report, vinyl album sales have increased more than 100 percent over the past ten years. Moreover, sales of vinyl records have grown for a twelfth consecutive year in 2017, and 14 percent of all album sales were on vinyl. But here is the real kicker: in spite of R&B/hip-hop becoming in 2017 for the first time the most dominant genre in music, with seven of the top ten albums coming from the genre, powered by a 72 percent increase in on-demand audio streaming, the top-selling vinyl LP of the year was not R&B/hip-hop. Rather, the top-selling vinyl LP of 2017 was the re-release of an album from a band in my parent's record collection: the Beatle's 1967 classic, *Sgt. Pepper's Lonely Hearts Club Band*.[4]

Moreover, in spite of the rise in on-demand audio streaming and the relatively low number of vinyl LPs sold today, it has been reported that "artists will make as much from the sale of 100 vinyl albums as they can from the 368,000 Spotify streams or 2.3 million YouTube views."[5] Consider this along with the fact that some contemporary artists, such as Daft Punk, Vampire Weekend, and Queens of the Stone Age, have first-week vinyl sales of 15,000 to 30,000 albums and that 70,000 to 80,000 copies of Jack White's *Blunderbuss* (2012) LP were pressed creates a demand now for more record plants,[6] which currently sit at around thirty total in the United States.[7]

Oddly enough, even though vinyl has enjoyed a resurgence over the past dozen years, I had no interest in increasing my record collection until a few years ago. I decided in the summer of 1997, after lugging my collection around in a move to a new city, that I would no longer purchase any more vinyl records or cassettes. Compact discs not only held more music, and were easy to find and inexpensive to purchase, but also didn't get eaten up in your player like cassette tapes and weren't heavy and bulky like records to store and transport. So I primarily acquired new music on compact disc and downsized both my record and cassette collections. Although I kept some vinyl around to spin, it was done more as an occasional homage to my listening past than an everyday practice of my listening present. Plus, many of my favorite LP records had been replaced by compact discs in my music library, so there was no reason to go back to vinyl—that is, until a few years ago.

The story here though begins in November of 2007, when I began writing regular essays on book culture for *American Book Review*. As fate would have it, I began my journey in writing on book culture the exact month that the first Kindle readers were released by Amazon—and sold out in just four and one-half hours. Just as vinyl record devotees believe the day that the first compact disc was pressed—August 17, 1982—was the beginning of the end of vinyl, I have explored the idea for a number of years that November 19, 2007—the day that the first Kindle readers were released— was the beginning of the end of the printed book.

These thoughts are primarily developed in two books, *Turning the Page: Book Culture in the Digital Age* (2014) and *The End of American Literature: Essays from the Late Age of Print* (2019). The general thesis of each is that book culture is transitioning from a print to a digital age. The essays in both focus on the political economy of books in this period of transition with regard to writers, readers, and publishers. But upon the completion of *The End of American Literature* in 2017, I began to notice that the transition from print to digital had lost some of its momentum. Prognostications of a digital utopia of books were losing steam, and printed books and even bookstores seemed to be enjoying a renaissance of sorts after being left for dead by the digital book euphoria of the early new millennium.

Nonetheless, as I noted above, since 2007, vinyl records have seen a resurgence. How could that be when even more so than printed books, vinyl records had virtually been abandoned by the consumer public twenty-five years earlier? So, while writing on and researching the transitions in the book industry and the philosophy of the book that underlies much of that discussion, I became interested in exploring parallel transitions in the record industry and the underlying philosophy of the record.

Vinyl Theory is the result of these explorations—although its central theses may be surprising to readers not familiar with the philosophy of the record and the political economy of music as established by critical theory. Unlike my work in *Turning the Page* and *The End of American Literature*, there is no writing through the present with regard to the vinyl record in this book. I note a few industry figures above regarding vinyl record and download sales to support the notion that vinyl records are making a comeback but do not prove it through an analysis of industry data.

Also, I ignore the commonplace argument that the return to vinyl is about nostalgia; for example, old-timers like me now have the disposable income to purchase all of that vinyl they could not afford in their youth. While sales figures can surely establish this point, the nostalgia argument does not lead to very interesting theoretical arguments about vinyl. Or, if it does, then a psychoanalytic account is probably the best direction here. I'd suggest a Lacanian approach, following through on Friedrich Kittler's idea of relating phonography, cinematography, and typing to Lacan's axiomatic registers of the real, the imaginary, and the symbolic. Its technological determinism may be appealing to some.[8]

In fact, although I have read and watched a number of entertaining accounts of the decline and/or resurgence of vinyl—most of which are largely centered on anecdotal comments by collectors, musicians, and record store owners and employees—none has really connected in any intriguing way the specificities of the material medium to our current political economy, that is, what is commonly termed *late capitalism* or *neoliberalism*.[9] *Vinyl Theory* is thus an effort to begin to bridge this gap.

The first chapter, "Late Capitalism on Vinyl," argues that we might view the fall and resurrection of vinyl over the course of the last twenty-five years as evidence of the resiliency of neoliberalism. It accomplishes this by examining the work of Friedrich Nietzsche and Jacques Attali on music through the lens of Michel Foucault's biopolitics, that is, the politics of life itself. The general aim of the chapter is to lay the groundwork for a twenty-first century biopolitics of music. It is a journey that begins in the late nineteenth century with Nietzsche and is extended from the same period through the work of Attali right through the late-seventies. It concludes with some observations as to how Attali's work understood as a pioneering work on biopolitics and the political economy of music contributes to our present concerns about the fall and resurrection of vinyl.

The second chapter, "The Curve of the Needle," focuses on Theodor W. Adorno's reflections on the phonographic record. As we shall see, Adorno's reflections on the phonographic record cover a wide range of topics including the listening habits of those who play records, the general character of the music put to vinyl and the record as a product of the culture industry. However, while these sociological observations on vinyl are certainly interesting and debatable ones, they are not the primary focus of this chapter. Rather, focus is placed here on Adorno's much deeper philosophical and phenomenological reflections on the phonograph, most of which were completed well before the advent of the long-playing record and the electric phonograph, namely, in the age of the short-playing (78 rpm[10]) record and the spring-driven non-electric gramophone.

My thesis in chapter 2 is that while the young Adorno was coming to philosophical terms with the "mechanized sound" of the gramophone, he was also reacting to the work of composers like Igor Stravinsky whose style of musical modernism he found reactionary and who also embraced both mechanical music and the phonographic record. These and other factors contributed to a lifelong disparagement of the phonograph, one that would continue unchanged even after major "improvements" were made to phonographic technology—a position he seemed to establish in advance of later changes in the technology. Nevertheless, in the year of his death, after a lifetime of sociological and philosophical dismissal of vinyl, he published a statement that would mark a surprising change in attitude toward vinyl.

Adorno is an important figure in vinyl theory because his critical theory coupled with his copious writing on music makes him our most prolific critical theorist of music. However, in spite of his many contributions to critical music theory, his theses regarding the biopolitics of music leave something to be desired compared to the work of Attali and others discussed in chapter 1. Still, as you will see, music cabinets like the one my parents had play an important role in his reflections on the sociology of the phonograph. So too do the jukebox records I bought in junior high.

Chapter 3, "It Might Get Loud," brings together Attali's theses about the role of sound control in social and political power and Adorno's concerns with the phonograph record to provide the setting for a unique role for sound control in the neoliberal economy: namely, the invention of high fidelity as a means of sustaining the political economy of music established by Attali. If Attali is right that what we call the "new economy"—late capitalism or neoliberalism—grew in strength along with the development of the record industry, then the invention of "high fidelity" was necessary to ensure that the authenticity issues alluded to by Adorno did not stunt the growth of both the record industry and neoliberalism.

I argue here that the recording studio became, in effect, "the control room" of neoliberalism. Spike Lee's film *Do the Right Thing* is used to show how resisting sound control—that is, "the control room"—has the potential to bring about social and political justice, but because there is a correlative relationship between sound control and economic control, the emancipatory potential of sound is limited. I conclude that if the illusion of high fidelity keeps the neoliberal economy chugging along, then the continuing practice of noise control protects it against failure, and only when it becomes loud, will we have a definitive sign that the neoliberal economy is in decline.

One of the things that I discovered in writing this chapter is that the authenticity issues I had at that KISS concert I saw in junior high have a long history in recorded music. Early ads for the phonograph reveal that tricking a live audience into believing that they were hearing live musicians rather than a phonograph was the gold standard of establishing the veracity of phonograph records. It is also, as I discuss in the chapter, linked to the invention of live music (and thus paving the way for albums like KISS's breakthrough 1975 album *Alive!*) by the record industry.

The final chapter, "Selling Out," employs the notion of selling out in the record industry to make some observations about the "theory industry." I argue that all theoretical sell outs are not the same: those who sell out theory through critique are doing the highest work of theory, whereas those who sell out theory as a means to personal, professional, or financial gain by sacrificing their critical integrity in an effort to become popular or successful, and forgetting their roots, are doing the lowest work of theory. The latter are so-called uncritical or neoliberal sell-outs, whereas the former are critical sell-outs. I use the Who's 1967 album *The Who Sell Out* to draw a parallel with the way Jacques Derrida sells out Western metaphysics in his 1967 theoretical trilogy, arguing that doing so posits a very high musical and theoretical bar for selling out.

In chapter 4, I argue that the basic moves of selling out music are similar to selling out theory. This argument is possible if we regard albums as comparable to books, articles to singles, and the classroom to a live performance. Cross-comparison of this sort allows for the development of a dialogue between the music industry and its academic counterpart. It is a dialogue that provides more clarity regarding both industries, especially when it comes to efforts to understand how, when, and why we sell out as theorists in particular and academics in general.

Vinyl Theory opens up some new directions for understanding the fall and resurrection of vinyl records. It also argues that the very existence of vinyl records may be central to understanding the resiliency of neoliberalism. The idea of writing this book came to me a few years ago when I could not believe that records were making a comeback. As I started listening to them more frequently again, I wondered how the political economy of music might be connected with the philosophy of the record. Literature on the latter topic is sparse though reaches its highest point in the work of Adorno, and speculation on the former is best represented by the work of Attali. What happens then when they are placed in dialogue in an effort to work toward a biopolitics of vinyl? This book is the result of the pursuit of these questions.

CHAPTER ONE

LATE CAPITALISM ON VINYL

Music has an incredible power over *life*. For some, music reveals this power through its ability to move our bodies and inspire our minds. Who cannot resist moving their hips when Chubby Checker asks us to do the twist? Or does not feel intellectually uplifted when listening to the music of J. S. Bach? Or politically committed and socially engaged when listening to Bob Dylan's "Hurricane" (1975), N.W.A.'s "Fuck Tha Police" (1988), or Public Enemy's "Fight the Power" (1989)?

For others though the connection between music and life is far stronger than mere affect. For people like Wolfgang Amadeus Mozart and Miles Davis, a case might be made that "music *is* life." Not just in the sense that their lives were consumed with making music, but also in a far stronger sense, namely, that for each of them "there is no life outside of music." Understanding what these two complementary statements might mean involves a consideration about the relations not just between life and music but also death and music. This also opens up a related question, that is, What is the capacity of music to *"foster* life" and to *"disallow* it to the point of death"?[1]

The composer of over six hundred works, including many of the most well-known and revered works of classical symphonic, operatic, concertante, choral, and chamber music, Mozart was a musical prodigy. Although he died at the age of thirty-five, almost all of these years involved musical composition in some form or another. For Mozart, it seems fair to say, music *was* his life. As a three-year-old, he watched his seven-year-old sister, Nannerl, take keyboard lessons with their father. After her brother's death, Nannerl reflected on Wolfgang's early interest in music: "He often spent much time at the clavier, picking out thirds, which he was ever striking, and his pleasure showed that it sounded good." "In the fourth year of his age his father, for a game as it were, began to teach him a few minuets and pieces at the clavier.... He could play it faultlessly and with the greatest delicacy, and keeping exactly in time.... At the age of five, he was already composing little pieces, which he played to his father who wrote them down."[2] In short, his brief life from his earliest years of age was completely consumed with music and its composition.

Although Miles Davis, like Mozart, had a parent who played violin and keyboard, Cleota Mae Henry Davis was not a composer or an experienced music teacher like Leopold Mozart.[3] Davis says in his autobiography that "[t]he first time I really paid attention to music was when I used to listen to a radio show called 'Harlem Rhythms.'" He "was about seven or eight" at the time, and then "when I was nine or ten I started taking some private music lessons."[4] Like Mozart, Davis was consumed with music. "When I got into music I went all the way into music; I didn't have no time after that for nothing else."[5] "By the time I was twelve," says Davis, "music had become the most important thing in my life."[6] Regarding a five-year period from 1975 to early 1980 during which Davis didn't pick up his horn even once, he comments, "I had been involved in music continuously since I was twelve or thirteen years old."[7]

It was all I thought about, all I lived for, all I completely loved. I had been obsessed with it for thirty-six or thirty-seven straight years, and at forty-nine years of age, I needed a break from it, needed another perspective on everything I was doing in order to make a clean start and pull my life back together again. I wanted to play music, but I wanted to play in big halls *all* the time instead of little jazz clubs. For the time being, I was through with playing little jazz clubs because my music and its requirements had just outgrown them.[8]

So, in the end, even the hiatus was about his life in music and finding a fresh perspective on it. "For me," writes Davis in summation in his autobiography, "music has been my life."[9]

For both Mozart and Davis, the *biopower* of music was something that they came to recognize and embrace from a very early age. They are examples of how music and life can be regarded as co-extensive and are illustrative of the extreme power of music over life. For most people, though, the power of music over life is far less overwhelming but many times no less significant. It can be observed in both the desire to dedicate one's life to musical performance and composition as well as in the enjoyment of listening to music and the accumulation of musical recordings. To be sure, the ways in which music exerts power over life are many—even if we are only now beginning to develop accounts of the biopolitics of music.

The power of music over life though goes well beyond the individual feelings and emotions of the performer, composer, and listener. Affect theory today encourages us to engage philosophical inquiries into aesthetic feeling in a dialogue with complementary areas such as psychology, neuroscience, biology, and cultural studies. It also pushes us beyond "tired" oppositions such as subject/object, mind/body, and nature/culture. Contemporary theorists explore affect as both a philosophical and a political problem, drawing material for their inquiries from philosophy, political theory, and everyday life.

For one such theorist, Brain Massumi, in a line of thought that can be traced back through Gilles Deleuze, Henri Bergson, and ultimately Benedict de Spinoza, we are immersed in affects. "Affect theory," writes Massumi, "does not reduce the mind to the body in the narrow, physical sense. It asserts that bodies think as they feel, on a level with their movements. This takes thinking out of the interiority of a psychological subject and puts it directly in the world: in the co-motion of relational encounter."[10] Massumi is concerned with intensities of experience related to an immediate participation in events of the world— a line of thought that "requires a far-reaching re-evaluation of what the body can do."[11] This re-evaluation has as its goal arriving "at a transformational matrix of concepts apt to continue the open-ended voyage of thinking-feeling life's processional qualities, foregrounding their proto-political dimension and the paths by which it comes to full expression in politics (taking the word in the plural)."[12] Affect moves through the "encounter" to "politics." Thus, his examination of the political dimensions of relational encounter is one of experience in-the-making and, as such, of a politics that is emergent.

In this chapter, I would like to acknowledge the importance of the work of Massumi and others on affect theory and note its potential for interesting and innovative work on a politics of music. Still, I am less interested here in a "proto-political" or an emergent politics of music than understanding the dominant political economy of music, which might alternately be labeled either neoliberal or late capitalist. Specifically, I ask how that politics engages the proposition that music has power over life. This particular politics is more attuned to the biopolitics of the late seventies and early eighties Michel Foucault than the work in the same period by Gilles Deleuze and Félix Guattari. The irony here is that whereas the latter wrote explicitly and eloquently about music during this period, the former did not.

In *A Thousand Plateaus: Capitalism and Schizophrenia* ([1980] 1987), although Deleuze and Guattari explain why music is so often concerned with death, their analysis is more about the problem of content and expression in music than the biopolitical economy of music or even its necropolitics, that is, the relationship between sovereignty and power over life and death. Still, the role of death as related to the content and expression of music is clearly stated:

> What does music deal with, what is the content indissociable from sound expression? It is hard to say, but it is something: *a* child dies, a child plays, a woman is born, a woman dies, a bird arrives, a bird flies off. We wish to say that these are not accidental themes in music (even if it is possible to multiply examples), much less imitative exercises; they are something essential. Why a child, a woman, a bird? It is because musical expression is inseparable from a becoming-woman, a becoming-child, a becoming-animal that constitutes its content.[13]

Thus, for Deleuze and Guattari music is often concerned with death "[b]ecause of the 'danger' inherent in any line that escapes, in any line of flight or creative deterritorialization: the danger of veering toward destruction, toward abolition."[14] Music confronts death "[n]ot as a function of the death instinct it allegedly awakens in us, but of a dimension proper to its sound assemblage, to its sound machine, the moment that must be confronted, the moment the transversal turns into a line of abolition."[15]

Music, for Deleuze and Guattari, "gives us a taste for death."[16] But this is very different from the idea that music can "disallow [life] to the point of death." It is this latter notion, following the biopower of Foucault, that I am most interested in pursuing. For Deleuze and Guattari, "music-making is expressive inasmuch as it serves to construct a territory."[17] And "[t]hat territory defends against the anxieties, fears, pressures we feel; it doesn't do away with them, of course, but gives them different form."[18] Although there is in the work of Deleuze and Guattari a direct and interesting response regarding the power of music over life and death, in this chapter, I would like to look at the more Foucauldian question of the power of music to both "foster life" and to "disallow it to the point of death" and its attendant or resulting political economy.

To engage music in a dialogue with power, life, and death is to engage it at a level where it becomes both a facet of biopower and a feature of biopolitics. But to do so is to go forward without the direct assistance of Foucault, who has very little to say about music in his work on biopower and biopolitics. Fortunately, however, his somewhat younger French contemporary, Jacques Attali, wrote at length about the biopolitics of music at the same time that Foucault was lecturing, with increasing depth, on biopolitics at the University of Paris in the mid- to late seventies. However, before examining Attali's contributions to a neoliberal biopolitics of music, I'd like to go back and reflect a bit on the work of a nineteenth-century philosopher who not only arguably made significant contributions to the biopolitics of music, particularly late in his career, but who is now becoming increasingly recognized as a thinker whose work on man as homo economicus is a prequel to our own neoliberal man. This thinker is of course the philosopher Friedrich Nietzsche.

My aim in examining the work of Nietzsche and Attali on music through the lens of Foucault's biopolitics is to lay the groundwork for a twenty-first-century biopolitics of music. It will be a journey that begins in the late nineteenth century with Nietzsche and is extended through the work of Attali into the late seventies. I'll conclude by making some observations as to how Attali's work understood as a pioneering work on biopolitics and the political economy of music contributes to our present concerns.

MUSIC CONTRA LIFE

Friedrich Nietzsche spent the fall of 1888 in Turin, Italy. During his stay, he went through his older writing going back as far as 1877 and selected pieces that reflected his position on the composer

Richard Wagner. The pieces, often shortened and clarified, were to become his final book, *Nietzsche contra Wagner*—a book that would not be published until many years later, that is, in 1895 in volume eight of his collected works.

Nietzsche wrote the preface for *Nietzsche contra Wagner* on Christmas of 1888, and then early the next month he became insane, after which his friend and former colleague, Overbeck, transported him back to Basel, Switzerland, from Turin. He was then committed to the asylum in Jena, Germany, but shortly thereafter released to the care of his mother in Naumburg, Germany. When his mother died in 1897, his sister moved him to Weimar, Germany, where he died on August 25, 1900.

Nietzsche contra Wagner leaves little doubt about his position on Wagner. "We are antipodes," writes Nietzsche in the preface, a position that he contends will not be a popular one with German readers. "I have readers everywhere," says Nietzsche, "in Vienna, in St. Petersburg, in Copenhagen and Stockholm, in Paris, in New York—I do *not* have them in Europe's shallows, Germany."[19]

His critique of the music of Wagner in this work and others is interesting both for what it is (a "physiological" one) and for what it is not (an "aesthetic" one). In fact, in the preface he alludes to this by saying that the book is "an essay for psychologists, but *not* for Germans."[20] Although Nietzsche "admire[s] Wagner wherever he puts himself into music," "[t]his does not mean that I consider this music healthy."[21] In brief, Nietzsche contends that the music of Wagner is not only unhealthy but also that the composer himself is a "sickness."

In *The Case of Wagner* [*Der Fall Wagner*], published in September of 1888 and the last book that Nietzsche would see to publication before his breakdown,[22] he is direct and clear about the effect of Wagner and his music on our health: "I am far from looking on guilelessly while this decadent corrupts our health—and music as well. Is Wagner a human being at all? Isn't he rather a sickness? He makes sick whatever he touches—*he has made music sick*—."[23]

Later, in the same section of *The Case of Wagner*, Nietzsche reflects further on the relationship between sickness, health, and life: "To sense that what is harmful is harmful, to be *able* to forbid oneself something harmful, is a sign of youth and vitality. The exhausted are *attracted* by what is harmful: the vegetarian by vegetables. Sickness itself can be a stimulant to life: one only has to be healthy enough for the stimulant."[24]

Health for Nietzsche involves a certain type of resilience, one that allows some people to "instinctively cho[ose] the *right* means against wretched states."[25] The resiliency of the healthy person enables that person to use sickness as a "stimulant to life." A variant of this line written in the same year (1888) from *Ecce Homo* links this all back to the development of a philosophy: "A typically healthy person, conversely, being sick can even become an energetic *stimulus* for life, for living *more*. This, in fact, is how that long period of sickness appears to me *now*: as it were, I discovered life anew, including myself; I tasted all good and even little things, as others cannot easily taste them—I turned my will to health, to *life*, into a philosophy."[26] The significance of these passages stems less with the German philosopher's specific problems with the music of Wagner or, for that matter, with vegetarianism (Wagner was a vegetarian, and Hitler is claimed to have followed the composer's dietary practice[27]) but rather with the way in which what we now call biopolitics enters into a dialogue with music through the late writing of Nietzsche.

Foucault first introduced the problematic of biopower in his lectures at the Collège de France in the spring of 1976 and then devoted his next two years of lectures at the Collège (the 1977/1978 and 1978/1979 academic years)[28] to developing his thoughts on biopolitics. In his final lecture in 1976 under the course title "Society Must Be Defended," he notes that in the second half of the eighteenth century "a new technology of power" emerges. He terms it here biopower and biopolitics.[29]

Foucault explains that while biopower "does not exclude

disciplinary technology . . . it does dovetail into it, integrate it, modify it to some extent, and above all, use it by sort of infiltrating it, embedding itself in existing disciplinary techniques."[30] "Unlike discipline, which is addressed to bodies," biopower "is applied not to man-as-body but to the living man, to man-as-living-being; ultimately, if you like, to man-as-species."[31] Biopower addresses "man-as-species" as "a global mass that is affected by overall processes characteristic of birth, death, production, illness, and so on."[32] It is a "seizure of power that is not individualizing but, if you like, massifying, that is directed not at man-as-body but at man-as-species."[33]

The first object of biopolitics are processes "such as the ratio of births to deaths, the rate of reproduction, the fertility of the population, and so on."[34] In the second half of the eighteenth century, biopolitics seeks to control these processes. It is here that "the first demographers begin to measure these phenomena in statistical terms."[35] During this period, death is "no longer something that suddenly swooped down on life—as in an epidemic."[36] Death becomes "permanent, something that slips into life, perpetually gnaws at it, diminishes it and weakens it."[37]

While Foucault enumerates many different elements that enter into the domain of biopolitics both in its early stages and its later stages, he says "biopolitics will derive its knowledge from, and define its power's field of intervention in terms of, the birth rate, the morality rate, various biological disabilities, and the effects of the environment."[38] Also, in addition, it "deals with the population, with the population as a political problem, as a problem that is at once scientific and political, as a biological problem and as power's problem."[39] Biopolitics is as well credited by Foucault with introducing "forecasts, statistical estimates, and overall measures."[40]

The topic of biopolitics is also discussed by Foucault around the same time in *The History of Sexuality: Volume I: An Introduction*, the 1978 English translation of his 1976 book *La volonté de savoir*. In part five of this book, entitled "Right of Death and Power over

Life," Foucault discusses "the ancient right to *take* life or *let* live" that comes to be replaced beginning in the eighteenth century by "a power to *foster* life or *disallow* it to the point of death."[41] The context here is the changes in the right of the sovereign to take life through the death penalty. Focus in the application of capital punishment shifts from the emphasizing the "enormity of the crime" to "the safeguard of society" and "the monstrosity of the criminal."[42] "Now it is over life, throughout its unfolding," comments Foucault, "that power establishes its dominion; death is power's limit, the moment that escapes it; death becomes the most secret aspect of existence, the most 'private.'"[43]

Under the aegis of an emerging biopolitics, "life more than the law . . . became the issue of political struggles"[44] to the point where even Aristotle's observations on the nature of man as a political animal were no longer valid. Whereas "[f]or millennia, man remained what he was for Aristotle: a living animal with the capacity for a political existence; modern man is an animal whose politics places his existence as a living being in question."[45]

It is against the relief of the emerging and developing biopolitics of the eighteenth and nineteenth centuries that Nietzsche's comments on the *life-giving* and *life-taking* powers of music begin to make more sense. While some might be inclined merely to dismiss Nietzsche's comments regarding Wagner's music as the aesthetic rantings of a philosopher whose well-known falling out with his former friend have tainted his appreciation of the composer, the emerging biopolitics indicated by Foucault provide an important and different context in which to understand his comments.

If Foucault is accurate in his assessment that the issue of measuring and calculating what fosters life and disallows it to the point of death is a major social and political preoccupation of the period, then Nietzsche's observations on the music of Wagner are prime fodder to begin a discussion of a *biopolitics of music*. For example, Nietzsche's comments that the music of Wagner is harmful to one's health and makes people sick might be understood through the context of the emerging social and political concerns and controls over the health of society. What might have seemed without bio-politics as a passing aesthetic jab at Wagner by Nietzsche becomes through the context of a biopolitics a commentary on the health of society. It also suggests that the philosopher's comment that *Nietzsche contra Wagner* is not a book for Germans and that he does not have readers in Germany entails that because the music of Wagner is championed in this country, its people, like the composer and his music, are sick and unhealthy.

Nietzsche explains in some detail in *Nietzsche contra Wagner* the difference between healthy and unhealthy music. It is a difference that is not grounded in aesthetics but rather in physiology. "My objections to the music of Wagner are physiological objections: why should I trouble to dress them up in aesthetic formulas? After all, aesthetics is nothing but a kind of applied physiology."[46] This notion of aesthetics as a "kind of applied physiology" turns up later in the twentieth century in efforts to measure the effects of music on people and to use these effects as a form of control over them.[47] For Nietzsche, however, the physiological "fact" of Wagner's music is quite clear: "My 'fact,' my *petit fait vrai*, is that I no longer breathe easily when this music begins to affect me; that my foot soon resents it and rebels: my foot feels the need for rhythm, dance, march—to Wagner's 'Kaiser-marsch' not even the young German Kaiser could march—it demands of music first of all those delights which are found in good walking, striding, dancing. But does not my stomach protest too? my heart? my circulation? Are not my entrails saddened? Do I not suddenly become hoarse? To listen to Wagner I need pastilles Gérandel [*sic*]."[48] It is important to note that Nietzsche's comments here are not about his emotional response to the music of Wagner but rather about its "affect."

Massumi clearly describes the difference—a difference that might be used to explicate Nietzsche's comment:

you have to understand affect as something other than simply a personal feeling. By "affect" I don't mean emotion in the everyday sense. The way I use it comes primarily from Spinoza. He talks of the body in terms of its capacity for affecting and being affected. These are not two different capacities—they always go together. When you affect something, you are at the same time opening yourself up to being affected in turn, and in a slightly different way than you might have been the moment before. You have made a transition, however slight. You have stepped over a threshold. Affect is this passing of a threshold, seen from the point of view of the change in capacity. It's crucial to remember that Spinoza uses this to talk about the body. What a body is, he says, is what it can do as it goes along.[49]

Thus, the problem with the music of Wagner according to Nietzsche is its affect on his body: it makes him breathe uneasily, upsets his stomach, pains his heart, changes the circulation of his blood, makes him so hoarse that he requires a throat lozenge (Pastilles Géraudel) to ease his physical discomfort.

The trouble here is that these are not the bodily affects Nietzsche "expects of music": "And so I ask myself: What is it that my whole body really expects of music? For there is no soul. I believe, its own *ease*: as if all animal functions should be quickened by easy, bold, exuberant, self-assured rhythms; as if iron, leaden life should lose its gravity through golden, tender, oil-smooth melodies. My melancholy wants to rest in hiding-places and abysses of *perfection*: that is why I need music. But Wagner makes sick."[50] The implications of Nietzsche's comments on the music of Wagner regarding a politics of life are manifest: music has power over life. Some music *eases* our body, whereas other music does the opposite, that is, *dis*-eases our body. This power of music over life extends to populations as well. It is, in the words of Foucault, "massifying." The fact that the people of Germany adore the music of Wagner is for Nietzsche a statement in itself on their overall health.

Although the "physiological objections" to the music of Wagner cited appear quite early in the philosopher's final book, *Nietzsche contra Wagner* (they are in the second section under the title "Where I Offer Objections"), they were first made in section 368 of *Die fröhliche Wissenschaft*, first published in 1882 and then again in a revised edition in 1887, whose title has been translated as *The Gay Science*. The wording is very similar to that in *Nietzsche contra Wagner*, but the philosopher noticeably omits the final paragraph of the section, which is stylistically set as a parenthetical reply from the Wagnerian: "(I forgot to mention how my enlightened Wagnerian replied to these physiological objections: 'Then you really are merely not healthy enough for our music?')."[51] This final thought in section 368 of *The Gay Science* brings us back to the matter of affect and capacity. Like Spinoza, Nietzsche views the body in terms of its capacity for affecting and being affected. However, Nietzsche's comments on Wagner open up the added dimension of considering the body in terms of its capacity for affecting music as well as its being affected by it. Thus, the question "Then you really are merely not healthy enough for our music?" arguably concerns both the domains of affect and biopolitics.

MODES OF MUSICAL PRODUCTION

A few weeks before Nietzsche's *The Case of Wagner* was published, a man named Charles Cros died in poverty. Cros, the author of *Kippered Herring* (*Hareng saur*) was also an inventor. Although his invention would ultimately not be a successful one, it was one of the earliest efforts to, in the words of another French theorist, "transform sound into writing, in other words, to achieve automatic stenography."[52] That theorist is Jacques Attali, and the invention was the "paleophone," one of the precursors to Thomas Edison's successful "automatic stenographer," the cylinder-based phonograph. Attali's book *Bruits: Essai sur l'économie politique de la musique* (1977)[53] shows how the invention of the phonograph brought about a new form of political economy, one he calls "repetition" but which we call today neoliberal political economy.

Bruits, translated into English by Brian Massumi in 1985 as *Noise: The Political Economy of Music,* takes its title from Attali's definition of music: "All music can be defined as noise given form according to a code (in other words, according to rules of arrangement and laws of succession, in a limited space of sounds) that is theoretically knowable to the listener."[54] His study is a primer of sorts on both biopower and biopolitics composed at the same time that Foucault was himself lecturing and publishing on the same topic. Moreover, and perhaps more important to the concerns of this chapter, Attali's *Bruits* provides an interesting historical framework in which to consider neoliberalism or neoliberal biopolitics in music.

Before *Bruits,* Attali published a few books on economic history, political economy, and political science including *La parole et l'outil* (1975), *Les modèles politiques* (1972), and *Analyse économique de la vie politique* (1972). And then, two years after, he published a book on the history of medicine, *L'ordre cannibale: Vie et mort de la médecine* (1979). His other book from this period was *La nouvelle économie française* (1978), published a year after *Bruits.* After the 1970s, however, Attali's writing production exploded, with well over sixty books to date authored by him. Although over half of these books are categorized like *Bruits* as "essays," his output includes at least five volumes of memoir, ten novels, five biographies (including studies of Diderot, Gandhi, Pascal, and Marx), two plays, two books of lyrics, two dictionaries, and a book of fairy tales. Still, in spite of his prodigious output, less than ten of his titles including *Bruits* have been translated into English: *A Man of Influence: The Extraordinary Career of S. G. Warburg* (1987); *Millennium: Winners and Losers in the Coming World Order* (1991); *A Brief History of the Future: A Brave and Controversial Look at the Twenty-First Century* (2009); *The Economic History of the Jewish People* (2010, with a foreword by Alan Dershowitz); *The Labyrinth in Culture and Society: Pathways to*

Wisdom (1998); *After the Crisis: How Did This Happen?* (2010); and *From Crystal to Smoke* (2010), his play about Kristallnacht.

However, the focus in this chapter is not on Attali the prolific public intellectual, who *Foreign Policy* magazine listed in 2008 and 2010 as one of the top 100 public intellectuals in the world,[55] but rather much more narrowly on how aspects of his early study *Bruits* provide an intriguing historical framework in which to discuss neoliberalism, or more precisely, neoliberal biopolitics, in music. Fredric Jameson, who wrote the foreword to the University of Minnesota Press translation, recognizes the neoliberal aspects of *Bruits*, writing "Attali's varied and complex reflections thus rejoin, from a unique perspective (which is, given his political role, a unity of theory and practice in its own right), the now widespread attempts to characterize the passage from older forms of capitalism (the market stage, the monopoly stage) to a new form."[56] The "unity of theory and practice" Jameson refers to is Attali's role as both an academic and practicing political advisor. A professor of economic theory at the École Polytechnique, the École Nationale des Ponts et Chaussées, and the Université Paris-Dauphine, Attali also served as a special adviser to the president of the republic (François Mitterand) from 1981 to 1991 and was the founder and first president of the European Bank for Reconstruction and Development in London from 1991 to 1993. Currently, he is CEO of A&A, an international consulting firm in strategy, based in Paris, and president of Positive Planet, an international non-profit organization assisting microfinance institutions all over the world, which as of the composition of this chapter advises and finances the development of microfinance in eighty countries.[57]

When Jameson wrote his foreword in 1985, Attali was already the author of a dozen books ranging from mathematical economy to health economics and music and recognized as "a central figure in France's . . . socialist experiment."[58] As Jameson notes, Attali's work including *Bruits* is written with "the sense that something new is emerging all around us, a new economic order in which new forms of cultural production can often give us the most precious symptoms, if not the prophetic annunciation."[59] Although Attali does not use terms like late capitalism or neoliberalism in his work to define this new form or stage of capitalism, retroactively we would term it as such. Jameson's foreword alludes to this: "This new form of capitalism, in which the media and multinational corporations play a major role, a shift on the technological level from the older modes of industrial production of the second Machine Revolution to the newer cybernetic, informational nuclear modes of some Third Machine Age. The theorists of this new 'great transformation' range from anti-Marxists like Daniel Bell to Marxists like Ernest Mandel (whose work *Late Capitalism* remains the most elaborate and original Marxian model of some new third stage of capital)."[60]

Jameson does a fine job of staging Attali's work in *Bruits* vis-à-vis the work of predecessors like Max Weber and Theodor Adorno but also of offering the ways in which it both comports with strictly linear historicist models of economic and social development by suggesting distinct stages as well as deviates from them. As a compliment to Attali's work, Jameson says that it avoids the historicist social staging of the work of contemporaries like Jean Baudrillard and Jean-François Lyotard, especially in a later work, *Les trois mondes* from 1981, in which he clearly "delinearizes" his proposed stages of social development, providing a type of synchronic and residual overlap with the socially dominant stage. His "three worlds" of representation in this 1981 work are "*regulation*, conceived in mechanical terms of determinism and reversibility— theory ultimately linked to the classical market"; "*production*, whose strong form is clearly classical Marxism"; and "*organization* of meanings and signs."[61]

In *Bruits*, Attali views music as "prophetic of the emergent social, political, and economic forms of a radically different society,"[62] arguing that there are four stages, or better yet, "networks," of music: sacrificing, representing, repeating, and composition. *Sacrificing* refers to the prehistory of modern music, the period prior to 1500 CE, a time before musical notation. During the sacrifice stage, music persists solely in the memory of people, most notably in oral songs and folktales. *Representing* refers to the area of printed music, roughly 1500 to 1900 CE. It is during this period that music becomes tied to a physical medium (printed music) and therefore becomes a commodity. For Attali, music "fetishized as a commodity . . . is illustrative of the evolution of our entire society: deritualize a social form, repress an activity of the body, specialize its practice, sell it as spectacle, generalize its consumption, then see to it that it is stockpiled until it loses meaning."[63]

Although his observations regarding the specific mode of production linked to sacrificing and representing are interesting, this chapter will focus on his third stage of music: *repeating*. This period begins with the invention of technologies of recording like those of Cros and Thomas Edison in the late nineteenth century and later broadcast sound and runs through the present. Here music is trapped and preserved on everything from discs covered with lampblack and wax cylinders to vinyl, tape, and compact disc. Although his final chapter hints at an emerging stage, *composition* (or simply, the post-repeating stage), his theory of it is incomplete and sketchy, particularly given the rich and extensive treatment given to the repeating stage. Still, the composition stage might be tied to modes of musical production associated with sampling, remixing, and live performance, but I'll leave speculation on it to another occasion and focus here on linking his work on repeating to what we might now call a *neoliberal biopolitics* of music. To do this though we need to go back now to Cros, Edison, and the late nineteenth century of Nietzsche.

RECORDING LATE CAPITALISM

"Recording has always been a means of social control," writes Attali. It allows power to not just "enact its legitimacy" but also stockpile memory of its power, a history that can be traced back to "the Tables of the Law."[64] But for Attali, it is not only power that is revolutionized through the "emergence of recording and stockpiling" but also music. For him, the revolution in recording and stockpiling "overturns *all* economic relations."[65]

In this new world of overturned economic relations, "the whole of understanding" is overturned as well. Although music is the first area where the processes of repetition are to be seen, science, particularly biological science, did not lag far behind music. "[T]he study of the conditions of the replication of life has led to a new scientific paradigm," comments Attali, one that "goes to the essence of the problems surrounding Western technology's transition from representation to repetition."[66] For him, this means that "[b]iology replaces mechanics."[67] The emergence of biology in the network of *repeating* or *repetition* coupled with the stockpiling of power through the revolution in recording provides us with the materials for a notion of biopower both comparable to and different from Foucault's.

Although the road to the emergence of a new form of power, biopower, goes through the transition of mechanics as the dominant science to biology, it does not start with a transformation in the natural sciences but rather with one in the applied physical sciences, namely developments in recording technology. And "with the appearance of the phonograph record, the relation between music and money starts to be flaunted, it ceases to be ambiguous and shameful."[68] For Attali, music is transformed into a unique type of commodity during the network of repetition. It is exemplary in this regard because it is "one of the first artistic endeavors truly to become a stockpileable consumer product."[69]

The phonograph record and its history are central to Attali's arguments about the emergence of a new economy. They lead him to talk less about the problem of content and expression in music (à la Deleuze) than about the biopolitical economy of music heralded by the development of new technologies of recording and stockpiling in the twentieth century. That is, Attali focuses more on the consumption of music and the industry that emerges in support of it.

For Attali, with the advent of recording, "music became an industry, and *its consumption ceased to be collective*. The hit parade, show business, the star system invade our daily lives and completely transform the status of musicians. Music announces the entry of the sign into the general economy and the conditions for shattering its representation."[70] The story of music becoming an industry is outlined by Attali by focusing on technological developments in the reproduction of sound and filtering them through a narrative that foregrounds the emergence of replication.

The birth of replication and its attendant neoliberal biopolitics begins with Cros's invention, the paleophone, one of several attempts prior to Thomas Edison's cylinder-based phonograph to preserve sound. Developed around 1861, Cros's paleophone was not taken seriously because he was not a specialist in the area. Writing sometime after he registered his invention with the Academy of Sciences in 1877, Cros complained,

> There is every reason to believe that they wanted to sidetrack me and I had the foresight to have my sealed envelope opened. . . . Justice will be done in the long run, perhaps, but in the meantime these things remain an example of the scientific tyranny of the capital. They express this tyranny by saying: theories float in the air and have no value, show us some experiments, some facts. And the money to run the experiments? And the money to go look at the facts? Get what you can. It is thus that many things are not carried out in France.[71]

Attali views Cros's failure here not as a scientific one but an economic one. Cros and others before Edison failed to "demonstrate the economic advantages" of transforming sound into writing. Even Edison, who patented his phonograph in 1877, lost interest in it the next year. The purpose of the phonograph, for Edison, "was to stabilize representation rather than to multiply it."[72] It was meant to be used as "an archival apparatus for exemplary words,"[73] a position supported by the fact that "speech was the only sound it was technically feasible to record before 1910, and even then only a few operas were recorded."[74] Attali notes that it was not until 1914 that the first symphony was recorded (Beethoven's Fifth, conducted by Arthur Nikisch).[75]

In short, no one foresaw during the late nineteenth and early twentieth century the mass production of music that was to come. Edison even went so far as to oppose the use of the phonograph in jukeboxes because it would make "it appear as though it were nothing more than a toy."[76] It was not until 1898, over twenty-two years after patenting his invention, that Edison "realized the commercial potential for recorded music."[77] It is important to note that it is in this context that Nietzsche is commenting on the life fostering and life enervating power of music, that is, in a context prior to its repetition through the phonograph.

So, in a way, the musical biopolitics of Nietzsche through the lens of Attali reference a different network of relations, namely, those of what he calls "representation." Through this network we can see music become a commodity, but it became one through a set of economic relations that would be overturned by "repetition," or what we now call neoliberalism.

The phonograph, along with the invention of radio and broadcast technology, for Attali, were "part of a radically new social and cultural space demolishing the earlier economic constructions of representation."[78] The phonograph came to be seen by conservatives in the early twentieth century "as something dangerous, giving a wide audience effortless access to a consumption of signs reserved for an elite."[79] Under the emerging conditions of repetition, the music of Wagner and Mozart undergo a "tremendous mutation."[80] Born in the age of representation, their music was something that people including the author of these works "perhaps did not hear more than once in a lifetime (as was the case with Beethoven's Ninth Symphony and the majority of Mozart's works)."[81] For Attali, "Mozart's works were almost exclusively background music for an elite who valued them only as a symbol of power."[82]

However, in the age of repetition, their work "becomes accessible to a multitude of people, and becomes repeatable outside the spectacle of its performance. It gains availability. It loses its festive and religious character as a simulacrum of sacrifice. It ceases to be a unique, exceptional event, heard once by a minority."[83] Attali's comments here remind us that much of Nietzsche's critique of the music of Wagner was linked to its religious character, particularly later works like *Parsifal* (1882). It also reminds us that outside of the opera houses that were staging these works, they were not heard by a mass audience. Attali's work thus points to a radical change in the biopolitics of music that occurred with the advent of the phonograph. One of the most significant is that it allows for the "stockpiling of time."[84]

According to Attali, "the first repetition of all was that of the instrument of exchange in the form of money. A precondition for representation, money contains exchange-time, summarizes and abstracts it: it transforms the concrete, lived time of negotiation and compromise into a supposedly stable sign of equivalence in order to establish and make people believe in the stability of the links between things and in the indisputable harmony of relations."[85] Recorded music, however, unlike money, contains *use-time*, not exchange-time. This is a crucial distinction for Attali. It allows him to show how a new economic process got underway with the "stockpiling of music." "It was thought that discourse—in other words, exchange-time once again—was being stockpiled, while in fact what was being stockpiled was coded noise with a specific ritual function, or use-time."[86] His point here is to distinguish music as a "unique commodity" because to take on meaning, it requires an incompressible lapse of time, that of its own duration. Thus the gramophone, conceived as a recorder to stockpile time, became instead its principal user. Conceived as a word preserver, it became a sound diffuser. The major contradiction of repetition is in evidence here: *people must devote their time to producing the means to buy recordings of other people's time*, losing in the process not only the use of their own time, but also the time required to use other people's time. Stockpiling becomes a substitute, not a preliminary condition, for use. *People buy more records than they can listen to. They stockpile what they want to find the time to hear.* Use-time and exchange-time destroy each other.[87]

In short, repetition "stockpiles use-time" and "Replicated man finds pleasure in stockpiling the instruments of deritualized substitute for sacrifice."[88] The notion of music as "stockpiling" is then also put to use by Attali to explain the presence of death in music.

Whereas for Deleuze and Guattari music "gives us a taste for death" and serves to construct a territory that defends against the anxieties, fears, pressures we feel, for Attali death "is present in the very structure of the repetitive economy: *the stockpiling of use-time in the commodity object is fundamentally a herald of death.*"[89] He writes, "it is no coincidence that many great musicians have chosen physical death (Janis Joplin, Jimi Hendrix, Jim Morrison), or institutional death (the Beatles). Or that theoretical music accepts noise and uncontrolled violence."[90] Why? Because repetitive society is an "age when death will be everywhere present."[91]

In a way, the biopolitics of music in Attali is more properly speaking a thanatopolitics, a politics of death, as music is the herald of death in a society where it is everywhere present including the structure of its economy. But repetitive distribution also fosters an ideal of health, or life, if you will. Repetitive distribution "has become a means of isolating, of preventing direct, localized, anecdotal, nonrepeatable communication, and of organizing the monologue of great organizations."[92] The political role of music, for Attali, is not found in "what it conveys, in its melodies or discourses, but in its very existence."[93]

"Power," he comments, "in its invading, deafening presence, can be calm: people no longer talk to one another. They speak neither of themselves nor of power. They hear the noises of the commodities into which their imaginary is collectively channeled, where their dreams of sociality and need for transcendence dwell. The musical ideal then almost becomes an ideal of health: quality, purity, the elimination of noises; silencing drives, deodorizing the body, emptying it of its needs, and reducing it to silence."[94] But what if everyone then decides to express themselves through this music? What then does it say about them? For Attali it says that "they have nothing more to say, because it no longer has a meaningful discourse to hold, because even the spectacle is now only one form of repetition among others, and perhaps an obsolete one. In this sense, music is meaningless, liquidating, the prelude to a cold social silence in which man will reach his culmination in repetition."[95] For Attali, the "absence of meaning . . . is nonsense; but it is also the possibility of any and all meaning."[96]

The final analysis of life in music under repetition is as follows: "If an excess of life is death, then noise is life, and the destruction of the old codes in the commodity is perhaps the necessary condition for real creativity."[97] The political power of music is not found in its lyrics or melodies but rather in the ways in which noise is controlled by society: "It is possible to judge the strength of political power by its legislation on noise and the effectiveness of its control over it . . . the history of noise control and its channelization says much about the political order that is being established today."[98] For Attali, the music of Dylan, N.W.A., and Public Enemy is no more or less political or powerful than any other music from this period, the late age of repetition.

CONCLUSION

In the final chapter, Attali's *Bruits* looks forward to a stage of music that avoids the commodification and exchange exemplary of repetition. This stage, termed *composition*, moves beyond repetition and its neoliberal biopolitics of music to something different. Attali's comments here on the characteristics of the post-repetition world regarding music are provisional. But more significant, they are not set in the material conditions of the technologies of music reproduction and distribution that would come to dominate the late 1990s and early twenty-first century, namely the digital revolution. Still, in spite of this, his analysis of repetition and its attendant neoliberal economy is extremely prescient.

In his 1978–79 lectures at the Collège de France, Foucault explains how neoliberals, at least in America anyway, "try to apply economic analysis to a series of objects, to domains of behavior or conduct which were not market forms of behavior or conduct; they attempt to apply economic analysis to marriage, the education of children, and criminality, for example."[99] For Foucault, this "poses a problem of both theory and method, the problem of applying such an economic model, the practical heuristic of the model, etcetera."[100] Foucault's comment here helps to situate Attali's analysis of the political economy of music in the twentieth century and to locate its difficulties.

Prior to the age of repetition, although music is a commodity, it does not really lend itself to market forms of behavior. It is only through the introduction of the phonograph that music becomes a market form of behavior but in doing so overturns the existing economic picture. In the process, *homo musicus* merges with *homo economicus*. And again, as Foucault points out in the same lecture series, "there are important stakes in the generalization of the grid of *homo economicus* to domains that are not immediately and directly economic."[101] The stakes, as Attali points out, turn out to be "the destruction of the old codes in the commodity," music, and the emptying of its meaning. Music under neoliberalism or late capitalism has more in common with death than life. Nietzsche's fears of the deadly impact of the music of Wagner become the fears of all music under late capitalism. The irony here of course was that Nietzsche too speculated on man as *homo economicus*, but because the technologies of music reproduction were only quietly developing during his lifetime, he could not foresee the ways in which the form of music consumption and distribution could be as life enervating as its content and expression.

My take on Attali's economic analysis of music in the twentieth century is that it is a dark road to neoliberal thought and biopolitics. In Foucault and Attali's work is the notion that neoliberalism revises what it means to be a human person, but the nature of that shift differs a bit. Foucault says that "[h]omo economicus is an entrepreneur, an entrepreneur of himself,"[102] whereas Attali seems to be qualifying this by insinuating that music in the twentieth-century facilitates *homo economicus* becoming an entrepreneur of himself. This idea is evident in Attali's comments on the exchange-time versus the use-time of music.

Foucault, citing Gary Becker, says that "[w]e should not think at all that consumption simply consists in being someone in a process of exchange who buys and makes a monetary exchange in order to obtain some products. The man of consumption is not one of the terms of exchange. The man of consumption, insofar as he consumes, is a producer. What does he produce? Well, quite simply, he produces his own satisfaction."[103] Perhaps we need to view the stockpiling of recorded music as both a unique form of commodity as well as one that through stockpiling allows for a new type of satisfaction or pleasure: the pleasure of stockpiling the instruments of deritualized substitute for sacrifice. Thus, Attali's "replicated man" can produce pleasure at will by simply spinning some vinyl or just collecting it.

Writing in the mid-seventies, Attali's analysis looks at a music industry that had already begun to move beyond vinyl with the advent of the eight-track and cassette tape as a means of stockpiling and distributing music. It describes the growth of this industry as characterized by an increasing dependence not only on the staples of neoliberal thought, namely, statistical methods and measurement, but also on the ways in which this technology changes both what economics means as well as what it means to be human.

So in light of Attali's thought, we might view the fall and resurrection of vinyl over the course of the last twenty-five years as evidence of the resiliency of neoliberalism. This observation is bad news for those who resist neoliberalism but collect records. Through the lens of Attali's work, this is analogous to being an animal rights advocate who also enjoys dining on a good steak. The good news though is that Attali's work gives us an excellent starting point to consider the resurgence of records and resiliency of neoliberalism.

CHAPTER TWO

THE CURVE OF THE NEEDLE

Igor Stravinsky was one of the first composers in the twentieth century to embrace the potential of the phonograph. Around 1928–29, Stravinsky signed a contract with the Columbia Gramophone Company to record his work as a pianist and composer. "This work greatly interested me," wrote Stravinsky in his autobiography completed in 1934, "for here, far better than with piano rolls, I was able to express all my intentions with real exactitude."[1] Not only did the composer find in the phonograph an ideal way to archive his own interpretations of his music, he also regarded musical recording for the phonograph as a way to supplement his own income.[2]

Still, in spite of touting its benefits for musical composers, he also had some doubts about those who use the phonograph to listen to music: "the evil of this so-called progress lies" in the "lack of necessity for any effort" that the gramophone requires of the listener. Writes Stravinsky, "anyone, living no matter where, has only to turn a knob or put on a record to hear what he likes," the ease of which leads some to then "listen without hearing."[3]

Perhaps there was no more outspoken opponent of the

gramophone during this early period of sound reproduction than the young Theodor W. Adorno, who began his published criticism of it in the late 1920s—and would continue right through his death in the late 1960s. For him, the gramophone encapsulated well the negative dialectics of modernity: the capacity to capture sound on vinyl was at once one of modernity's most remarkable technical achievements and also one of the music world's most disappointing developments. For Adorno, the invention of the gramophone paved the way for the commodification of music through the phonographic record. Moreover, the music that came to be commodified (or "canned" as Adorno says in our epigraph) was mass art that resisted musical innovation. It was music that did not require "listening," or in Adorno's terms, was "popular music" wherein "[t]he composition hears for the listener."⁴ The music that resisted "commodification" and "canning" was the autonomous art or "serious music" that was unsuited to the technical capacities of the phonograph.

Adorno's writing on the topic of the phonograph primarily focused on the negative aspects of music's adaptation to reproduction. He repeatedly insisted that the technical capacities of musical recording and sound reproduction were simply insufficient to meet the needs of the music he critically championed, namely, "serious music," from Beethoven to Berg—even though musical recording and sound reproduction in the age of vinyl was more than sufficient to serve the ends of the "popular music" he loathed. To put an even finer point on this distinction, we might alternately say that the phonograph for Adorno was more than capable of meeting the demands of "music which accepts its character as a commodity, thus becoming identical with the machinations of the culture industry itself" but did not meet the demands of "self-reflexive music which critically opposes its fate as a commodity, and thus ends up by alienating itself from present society by becoming unacceptable to it."⁵

It should be noted though that Adorno does not completely lay blame for "popular music" on the phonograph and the music industry that grew from it. For him, the kind of music produced by the culture industry through the phonograph "probably" pre-existed its invention—at least in rudimentary form: "The stagnation of the culture industry is probably not the result of monopolization, but was a property of so-called entertainment from the first. Kitsch is composed of that structure of invariables which the philosophical lie ascribes to its solemn designs. On principle, nothing in them must change, since the whole mischief is intended to hammer into men that nothing must change."[6] But, as we shall see, Adorno's reflections on the phonographic record extended well beyond just the general character of the music put to vinyl and the record as a product of the culture industry. These topics as well as the listening habits of those who played records were of course discussed by him and are certainly interesting and debatable ones. However, in addition to these sociological observations on vinyl, Adorno also contributed a much deeper philosophical and phenomenological set of reflections, most of which were completed well before the advent of the long-playing record and the electric phonograph. To be sure, Adorno's major philosophical reflections on the phonograph were completed in the age of the short-playing (78 rpm) record and the spring-driven non-electric gramophone.

My thesis here is that these deep philosophical reflections of the young Adorno coming to terms with the "mechanized sound" of the gramophone coupled with the fact that composers such as Stravinsky—whose style of musical modernism he found reactionary[7]—embraced mechanical music and the phonographic record contributed along with other factors to a lifelong disparagement of the phonograph. This disparagement would continue unchanged even after major improvements were made to phonographic technology—a position he seemed to establish in advance of later changes in the technology. Finally, after a lifetime of sociological and philosophical dismissal of vinyl, he published a statement in the year of his death that would mark a surprising change in attitude regarding vinyl. But let's not get too ahead of ourselves.

THE WORDS OF A COMPOSER

In the twenty-volume German collected edition of Adorno's work, over four thousand of its roughly ten thousand pages are given to the topic of music. Principal among this work are his books *Philosophy of Modern Music* (1949), *In Search of Wagner* (1952), *Dissonanzen* (1956), *Sound Figures* (1959), *Mahler: A Musical Physiognomy* (1960), *Introduction to the Sociology of Music* (1962), *Der getreue Korrepetitor* (1963), *Quasi una Fantasia: Essays on Modern Music* (1963), *Moments musicaux* (1964), *Alban Berg: Master of the Smallest Link* (1968), and *Impromptus* (1968), which all appeared during his lifetime, as well as *Beethoven: The Philosophy of Music* (1993), *Towards a Theory of Musical Reproduction* (2006), and *Current of Music* (2009), which were published posthumously.

In these works and many others, Adorno writes about nearly every aspect of the world of music: composers from Bach and Beethoven to Berg and Boulez, compositions ranging from chamber and orchestral music to opera, compositional procedure, conductors and conducting, musical form, musical listening, musical nationalism, musical pedagogy, musical performances, new music, popular and light music, jazz, kitsch, radio music, recording technology, the role of the critic in music, and on and on. To be sure, no other twentieth-century philosopher has written as much about music or covered so many specific aspects of it as Adorno.

In addition, it should not be forgotten that Adorno was not only a philosopher of music and a music critic but also a respectable music composer himself. In his youth, he entertained the idea of becoming a composer and concert pianist and even took piano lessons with Bernhard Sekles, who was also the teacher of the composer Paul Hindemith. In 1925, when he was only twenty-two years old, Adorno moved to Vienna where he became a composition student of Alban Berg and took piano lessons from Eduard Steuermann,[8] who along with Berg was a member of Arnold Schoenberg's circle.[9] Of Adorno's First String Quartet, composed during this period, Berg wrote to Schoenberg that it is "very good and I believe would meet with your approval."[10] Adorno would go on to compose music for most of his adult life, including an unfinished opera based on the writings of Mark Twain.[11]

However, of these one million words about music, only three very short essays are devoted to the principal means of its mechanical or technological reproduction in the twentieth century: the phonograph and the phonographic record. Two were written very early in his career—the first when he was in his mid-twenties and the second in his early thirties—and the last was published in the year of his death. This means that the philosopher who famously introduced (along with Max Horkheimer) the world to "the culture industry"[12] and discussed "[a]musement under late capitalism"[13] in *Dialectic of Enlightenment* in 1944, and whose work was dominated by the critical analysis of music, largely ignored directly addressing not only the phonographic record and the technology of phonographic recording but also the industry built upon these technologies, namely the record industry. This, however, is not to say that he did not write extensively about the music that was put to record; nor is it to say that he did not extensively speculate on other technologies of music reproduction, such as radio. Rather, it is to say that his work by and large, dismissed early both the record as a viable means of music reproduction and the record industry as a legitimate source for "serious music."[14]

This lack creates a strange void in his work on music—albeit one that can perhaps only be understood by examining his approach to and reflections on the phonograph and the phonographic record as stated in these three remarkable essays, which form his aesthetic triptych on the phonograph. On the one hand, no critical thinker has more extensively examined the composition and development of modern music in the twentieth century than Adorno; on the other hand, although he identifies a role for music under late capitalism, his examination of its political economy vis-à-vis twentieth-century advances in the technology of its reproduction is arguably severely underdeveloped. This lack of development is clear especially when compared, for example, to the work of Attali, one of his successors, who, as we saw in the previous chapter, used the development of sound recording in the twentieth century to situate the record album at the center of the emerging new economy, late capitalism. I think this becomes particularly evident when Adorno's work on the phonographic record is played *backwards* against the work of Attali, who in his book, *Bruits: Essai sur l'économie politique de la musique*, published eight years after Adorno's death, shows how the invention of the phonograph brought about a new form of political economy, one he calls "repetition" but which we call today "neoliberal" political economy.

Adorno, however, as we shall see, does not take his own reflections on the record as far as Attali. Although the advent and growth of phonographic recording plays a large role in determining how we consume music, and the impact of the phonograph on musical consumption also affects the production of music, Adorno stops far short of Attali's conclusion that the invention of the phonograph brought about a new form of political economy. Rather, for Adorno, whereas "music underwrote the principle of consumerism during the early heyday of the Industrial Revolution that anchored commonplace understanding of the very nature of modernity,"[15] its reproduction on vinyl did not, as Attali argues, usher in postmodernity and a new form of political economy, namely, what has come to be known as neoliberalism or late capitalism.

Records and the industry that produces them, for Adorno, function as a species of "amusement" under late capitalism: "Amusement under late capitalism is the prolongation of work. It is sought after as an escape from the mechanized work process, and to recruit strength in order to be able to cope with it again. But at the same time mechanization has such power over man's leisure and happiness, and so profoundly determines the manufacture of amusement goods, that his experiences are inevitably afterimages of the work process itself."[16] That Adorno will early on regard the phonograph as the mechanization of music or "mechanical music" only contributes to the later disdain he has toward the phonographic record.

As an example of how the phonograph "underwrote the principle of consumerism during the early heyday of the Industrial Revolution," Adorno commentator Richard Leppert asks us to consider "the history of piano design, manufacture, and distribution in the course of the nineteenth century," which he regards as a "perfect metaphor of capitalist economic principles in operation" and "an agent of capitalism's political, economic, and ideological success":

> Manufactured on a massive scale for a seemingly insatiable audience of consumers, the domestic piano bespoke a principal contradiction on nineteenth-century bourgeois society. High-caste pianos with elaborately decorated cases virtually fetishized conspicuous materialism; at the same time the music to be played on the instrument was valorized precisely because of its immateriality, to the nineteenth century the sine qua non of music's supposedly socially transcendent autonomy. Whatever its aesthetic correlates, the piano was a consumer product whose presence helped to define familial prestige akin to that of today's family-room "entertainment centers," not for nothing so-named, in advertising lingo that teaches us to focus our eyes on the screen and ears on the speakers to learn what's for sale, in exchange for the shows and music that come along as loss leaders.[17]

It is in much the same way that Adorno came to view the phonograph and the phonographic record: namely, as metaphor for capitalist economic principles in operation—and not, with Attali, as determinant of a new form of political economy.

In short, for Adorno, the phonograph and the phonographic record not only underwrote the principle of consumerism that anchored the commonplace understanding of the very nature of modernity; it was also typical of the kind of amusement functioning under late capitalism. Let's now look at each of Adorno's three essays on the phonograph in turn and see his thoughts on the technology that made music into a commodity.

THE CURVES OF A NEEDLE

When Adorno went to Vienna in 1925 to study composition with Alban Berg, he was just twenty-two years old. In the same year, he started to contribute essays on music to *Musikblätter des Anbruch*, an avant-garde music journal founded in Vienna in 1919. Berg was the first editor of the journal and presumably established his student's connection with the journal. It was here that he first began to work out in print his thoughts on music, culture, and technology.

In 1929, after four years as a frequent contributor to the journal, Adorno was put on its editorial board. One of his first contributions was to change the title to simply *Anbruch*. At the same time, he also initiated an attack on the reactionary forces in the music world and broadened the scope of the journal to include "light music" and kitsch. In fact, one of the first issues of *Anbruch* was entirely devoted to the subject of "light music." Its contributors included Ernst Bloch, Ernst Krenek, Kurt Weill, and Adorno, who wrote an essay on three popular hit tunes of the day. Other topics covered in the issue included operettas, film music, salon orchestras, and radio.[18]

Adorno early on recognized the importance of studying the complete range of musical production and not just the so-called serious music. In "Zum *Anbruch*: Exposé," an unpublished manuscript from 1928, he writes,

> In conjunction with sociological analyses there is also an entire field of music—previously denied any serious study whatsoever— which ought to be incorporated into the domain of *Anbruch*; namely, the entire realm of "light music," of kitsch, not only jazz but also the European operetta, the hit tune, etc. In doing so, one

ought to adopt a very particular kind of approach that ought to be circumscribed in two senses. On the one hand, one must abandon the arrogance characteristic of an understanding of "serious" music which believes it can completely ignore the music which today constitutes the only musical material consumed by the vast majority of people. Kitsch must be played out and defended against everything that is merely elevated mediocre art, against the now rotten ideals of personality, culture, etc. On the other hand, however, one must not fall prey to the tendency—all too fashionable these days, above all in Berlin—to simply glorify kitsch and consider it the true art of the epoch merely because of its popularity.[19]

So, well before his work with Horkheimer on "the culture industry," Adorno was grappling on his own with aspects of this later critique. Here kitsch is both defended against immediate dismissal but at the same time not simply glorified because of its popularity.

Adorno also recognized in this early work that consideration of the technologies of music cannot be disregarded in the study of music. To this end, he proposed that *Anbruch* include a section dedicated to the subject of music and machines, namely, "Mechanische Music." In its previous incarnation as *Musikblätter des Anbruch*, the journal had a feature oriented toward "the *producers* of mechanical music, i.e., the record industry, the gramophone manufacturers, etc., in hopes of attracting advertising,"[20] but because the manufacturers had their own trade journals, the advertisement revenue never materialized, so the journal dropped the feature. Writes Adorno,

The purpose of the rubric on mechanical [music] is not merely to trace journalistically a conspicuous trend in current musical life. Rather, it will attempt to shed light on the meaning of mechanization, will weigh the different tendencies of mechanization against each other and will try to have an influence on the politics of programming. All of this grows out of the conviction that the mechanical presentation of music today is of contemporary relevance in a deeper sense than merely being currently available as a new technological means. To put it another way, this position arises out of the conviction that the availability of means corresponds to an availability of consciousness and that the current historical state of the works themselves to a large extent requires them to be presented mechanically.[21]

For Adorno, the category of mechanical music is a "trend" that includes radio broadcasts, phonographic records, and film scores for both silent and sound film. Thus, this *Anbruch* forum on mechanical music was directed toward providing consumers of these various sound media technical and musicological advice on its usage—albeit, and most importantly, not as an "advertising stooge" for the gramophone industry (like a trade journal).

Within this context of widening the scope of what is considered popular music, while suggesting that technological trends were an important part of music criticism, Adorno engages in the first of his three major expositions on the gramophone. The essay, "Nadelkurven," translated as "The Curves of the Needle," was written in 1927 and first published in *Musikblätter des Anbruch* in February 1928, well before Adorno joined its editorial board.[22] It was again reprinted in *Phono: Internationale Schallplatten-Zeitschrift* in 1965 though with slight revisions and this important note from Adorno: "It goes without saying that over the course of forty years, insights into a technological medium become outdated. On the other hand, even at that time there was already a recognition of aspects of the transformed character of experience which, even as it was caused by technology, also had an effect on that very same technology. The motifs have been retained unchanged and with no attempt to cover up the temporal distance; the author made changes in the language to the extent that he deemed it necessary."[23] In many ways, this note is the place to begin regarding Adorno's thoughts on this technological medium because in it he admits that for the most part his views on the phonograph and phonographic record-ings have remained the same in the forty years since he wrote the essay. Although the technology of the medium had changed over time, the motifs he related to the phonograph in 1927 (and then again a few years later) remain unchanged in 1965. What then are these motifs? The following are those I understand to be the six major ones found in this particular essay; the next two sections identify additional ones found in the other two essays.

1. The phonographic record is comparable to the photograph. According to Adorno, in the early stages of photographic tech-nology (e.g., the daguerreotype), it "had the power to penetrate rationally the reigning artistic practice." However, as soon as one "attempts to improve these early technologies through an empha-sis on concrete fidelity, the exactness one has ascribed to them is exposed as an illusion by the very technology itself."[24] He believes that the same holds for the phonograph: the more "recordings become more perfect in terms of plasticity and volume, the sub-tlety of color and the authenticity of vocal sound declines as if the singer were being distanced more and more from the apparatus."[25] For Adorno, "the transition from artisanal to industrial production transforms not only the technology of distribution but also that which is distributed."[26] In short, as technology works to improve sound fidelity, sound authenticity declines proportionally. Adorno was not interested in accounting for the changes in sound record-ing technology over the forty-year span of the republication of his essay because he believed such advances only further confirmed what he said in 1927: that is, records were on the decline ever since the invention of the "talking machine."

Today it is difficult not to read Adorno's comments here through the lens of Walter Benjamin's 1936 essay "The Work of Art in the Age of Mechanical Reproduction,"[27] especially since Adorno was Benjamin's "first and only disciple."[28] But unlike Benjamin who bemoans the loss of "aura" in the mechanical reproduction of art, Adorno seems to be saying something a bit different here, namely, that advances in photographic and phonographic technology only serve to deteriorate the "indexical" relationship among the sign, its object, and its interpreter. As recording technology improves, the indexical relationship between the music performed (the object) and its recording (the representamen) degenerates for its listeners (the interpretant).[29]

Later, however, he literally mimics the voice of Benjamin, commenting in 1940, "[n]ow, we believe that *this* authenticity, or aura, is vanishing in music because of mechanical reproduction. The phonograph record destroys the 'now' of the live performance and, in a way, its 'here' as well."[30] Nevertheless, regardless of how you theoretically formalize Adorno's remarks here, his message is the same: technological progress in phonograph sound reproduction is inversely proportional to the quality of the listening experience.

2. "The relevance of talking machines is debatable." This line is so important that Adorno repeats it verbatim twice in "Nadelkurven." He views the phonograph as a "utensil of the private life that regulates the consumption of art."[31] Key to this regulation is that some music reproduces better on the phonograph than other music. "For the time being, Beethoven defies the gramophone," comments Adorno. "The diffuse and atmospheric comfort of the small but bright gramophone sound corresponds to the humming gaslight and is not entirely foreign to the whistling teakettle of bygone literature."[32] In other words, because the range of music that can be authentically reproduced on the phonograph is limited—it can reproduce "popular music," for example, "light music," kitsch, jazz, the hit tune, etc., authentically but not "serious music," for example, Beethoven—its relevance is debatable.

3. The phonograph has become a status symbol. Just as the piano was transformed "from a musical instrument to a piece bourgeois furniture,"[33] so too has the phonograph been transformed but only "in an extraordinarily more rapid fashion."[34] "In the functional salon, the gramophone stands innocuously as a little mahogany cabinet on little rococo legs," reports Adorno. "Its cover provides a space for the artistic photograph of the divorced wife with the baby," he cleverly continues, drawing our attention back to the similarities between the fate of the photograph and that of the phonograph. He mocks those who as "the expert examines all the needles and chooses the best one," while others who cannot afford to own their own phonograph, let alone a high-end phonograph, "just drops in his dime [into the jukebox]," saying that "the sound that responds to both [the actions of the expert and the jukebox user] may well be the same."[35] Here the social status of owning an expensive phonograph is undermined by his assertion that even those who cannot afford this luxury can still experience the same sound fidelity albeit for a fraction of the cost. In short, again, Adorno sees in the phonograph a metaphor for *capitalist* economic principles in operation—not serious *musical* ones.

4. Records allow us to hear ourselves. Adorno speaks of the "primordial affect which the gramophone stimulated and which perhaps even gave rise to the gramophone in the first place."[36] This "primordial affect," which he refers to as "the mirror function of the gramophone,"[37] is its ability to allow the listener to hear himself. "What the gramophone listener actually wants to hear is himself," writes Adorno. The musical artist offers to the listener through the phonograph record "a substitute for the sounding image of his own person." As such, when records perform this "mirror function," they become "virtual photographs of their owners, flattering photographs—ideologies." Even if the primary function of records is to archive sound or sound images of musical art, their "primordial affect" is to preserve their listeners. Records are valuable to their listeners because they are a means for the listeners to "possess" or own themselves. Thus, when we safeguard records, we are safeguarding ourselves. "The only reason that he [the possessor of a record] accords the record such value is because he himself could also be just as well preserved."[38]

This, of course, is an obvious nod to Jacques Lacan's well-known "mirror stage," during which the child gains its first sense of identity. But, as with Benjamin's famous essay noted above, Lacan's "The Mirror Stage as Formative of the *I* Function, as Revealed in Psychoanalytic Experience" was also published well after Adorno's work here—in 1949, over twenty years later.[39] So too is Adorno's mention of the record's connection with the "ideologies" of their listeners a nod to Lacan, for as one of the psychoanalyst's commentators put it, "the mirror stage is our initial imaginary gateway to the ongoing operations of normativity that help put the 'I' in ideology and keep ideology in the 'I.'"[40] Adorno thinks that the HMV record logo where the dog "Nipper" is seen listening to his master's voice through the gramophone horn is the "right emblem" for the mirroring function of records. Presumably, just as we can hear our own sound image in our records, so too can our dog, who primarily communicates with us through our sound images. Needless to say, the mirroring function of records only works *if* there are sound images available on vinyl that are representative of the listener's ideology. But what happens when these sound images are not available on record?

5. The mechanical reproduction of sound is limited. The technology of the phonograph is limited in its ability to perform the mirror function. Comments Adorno, "[w]hat is best reproduced gramophonically is the singing voice."[41] However, "[m]ale voices can be reproduced better than female voices."[42] By "best" Adorno means "most faithful to the natural ur-image and not at all most appropriate to the mechanical from the outset."[43] Thus, on the one hand, the gramophone gives "every female voice a sound that is needy and incomplete," while, on the other hand, the capacities of gramophonic technology explain "Caruso's uncontested dominance."[44] But just as there are limits to vocal reproduction by the gramophone, so too does "absolute pitch run into difficulties."[45] "It is almost impossible," by listening to a record, "to guess the actual pitch if it deviates from the original one."[46] As such, "the original pitch becomes confused with that of the phonographic reproduction."[47]

These mechanical limitations negatively impact both the relevance of the phonograph and its ability to perform widely the mirror function. A very limited vehicle of mechanical sound reproduction, Adorno's phenomenological assessment of the phonograph here leaves very little room for it to have a positive impact on either listeners or music appreciation.

6. Records are like empty clay pots. Adorno compares the turntable to the potter's wheel as both produce a *Ton-Masse*.[48] The German word for "clay" is "Ton." But it is also the word for "tone" or "sound." This word, *Ton-Masse*, thus allows Adorno to bring together the spinning motion of both tables in one compound word. Thus, in the final analysis of the young Adorno, the "turntable of the talking machines is comparable to the potter's wheel," which begins by spinning a "clay mass."[49] When finished, the clay container that is produced is empty until it is filled by a user. The same goes for records: the turntable begins by spinning a "sound mass" or "tone mass," that is, a record. However, the record, like the clay container produced by the potter's wheel, is empty until it is "filled by the hearer."

In sum, each these six motifs are the heart of the young composer's reflections on the phonograph. And each, of course, just touch the surface of deeper and more complex sets of issues he has with phonographic records in general. What is clear though from this initial set of motifs is that Adorno is not very impressed with the mechanization of sound reproduction via the phonograph—and that this early work sets the stage well for a lifetime of negative comments about the phonograph.

THE FORM OF A RECORD

Adorno would not write another piece explicitly on the phonograph record for another seven years—and even then, it would be published under a pseudonym. The essay, "Die Form der Schallplatte," translated as "The Form of the Phonographic Record," was published in 1934 in the journal *23: Eine Wiener Musikzeitschrift,* which was founded a few years earlier in 1932.[50] The journal takes its title from paragraph 23 of Austrian journalism law, which guarantees the right to force publication of corrections to falsely published information. Although established to provide rigorous music criticism as a "corrective" to unrigorous music criticism, it quickly widened its scope beyond just music criticism.[51] Presumably, given the controversial nature of the journal, Adorno opted to publish his essay under the name "Hektor Rottweiler."[52]

Although some of the motifs addressed in "The Curves of the Needle" are again taken up in "The Form of the Phonograph Record"—for example, the comparisons of the phonograph to photography and the limits of the mechanical reproduction of sound—new motifs are taken up, and there is a distinctly different approach to this later essay. As for the similarities, there are again comparisons of the photograph to phonographic recording but with a slightly different emphasis. Here, Adorno comments that because phonograph records were "spared the artisanal transfiguration of artistic specificity," they have remained "nothing more than the acoustic photographs that the dog [viz., the dog "Nipper" in the HMV record logo who is seen listening to his master's voice through the gramophone horn] so happily recognizes."[53] Moreover, record collecting is compared to photograph collecting: "records are possessed like photographs; the nineteenth century had good reasons for coming up with phonograph record albums alongside photographic and postage-stamp albums, all of them herbaria of artificial life that are present in the smallest space and ready to conjure up every recollection that would otherwise be mercilessly shredded between the haste and hum-drum of private life."[54]

The comment that records have been "spared the artisanal transfiguration of artistic specificity" refers to the claim that as of 1934, "[t]here has been no development of phonographic composers" and there "has never been any gramophone-specific music."[55] Specifically, he calls out Stravinsky in this context, saying "despite all his good will towards the electric piano, [he] has not made any effort in this direction." Consequently, because the phonograph has not played any role in musical composition, "the phonograph record is not good for much more than reproducing and storing a music deprived of its best dimension, a music, namely, that was already in existence before the phonograph record and is not significantly altered by it."[56]

Adorno calls out Stravinsky because of his long-standing interest in mechanical music. In 1917, Stravinsky wrote a specific piece of music for the pianola, and in 1923, he signed a six-year contract to record his entire corpus on pianola rolls[57]—and, as mentioned earlier, a few years later signed another contract to put his entire oeuvre on phonograph record. It should be noted that the pianola, later called the "player piano," was patented in 1897. The early pianola was a cabinet with wooden "fingers" projecting from it that was stationed in front of an ordinary piano. A paper roll activated the fingers to play the recorded music. This technology still exists with digital memory replacing the paper rolls.

In the early twentieth century, these pianolas could reproduce performances by Claude Debussy, Sergey Rachmaninoff, Artur Rubinstein, and George Gershwin. Later versions could even capture nuances of playing such as tempo change, crescendos, and other dynamics. They would come to be called "reproducing pianos." Player piano technology developed more or less simultaneously with phonograph technology. Early development of the player piano was roughly contemporaneous with the early development of the phonograph and dates back to Frenchman Henri Fourneaux's invention of the "pianista" in 1863.[58]

Later, in 1930, four years before Adorno's essay, Stravinsky wrote in "My Position on the Phonograph Record," "it would be of the greatest interest to produce music specifically for phonographic reproduction, a music which would only attain its true image—its original sound—through the mechanical production." "This," he continues, "is probably the ultimate goal for the gramophonic composer of the future."[59] But the expectation of using the phonograph as an artisanal element in music composition is more Adorno "the composer" speaking rather than Adorno "the philosopher," as the same comment could be made for all mechanisms of sound reproduction from radio transmission to digital reproduction.

As to the limits of sound reproduction, he goes nowhere into the depth of the earlier essay but does note that "the inevitable brevity dictated by the size of the vinyl plate" makes it "too sparse for the first movement of the Eroica [viz., Beethoven's Third Symphony] to be allowed to unfold without interruption."[60] Much later, as we shall see below, the capacity to put lengthier pieces of music on one side of a record, more than anything else, leads Adorno to reverse course on his general opinion of phonograph records. But in the earlier context of the shorter-playing records of the early 1930s, this comment is developed within the context of a set of remarks about the "thingness" of records—a motif not developed in the earlier essay.

7. The phonographic record allows us for the first time to possess music like a thing. But Adorno is clear that the need or desire to possess music like a thing is one that had to be developed and is not a "human requirement" or "human need." "[O]nce the thing [that is, the phonographic record] already exists and is spinning in its own orbit," the "need" for it "is initially produced by advertisement."[61] In other words, although advertising has convinced us that we need to possess music like a thing, we don't really need records. Phonographic recordings may be a technological marvel, but they are not a response to human needs. It is here that Adorno establishes the role of modernity and modernization in the development of the phonographic record.

8. The phonographic record is a product of modernity, not human need. For Adorno, the record is one of the first of the technological artistic-inventions of modernity. It "stems from an era that cynically acknowledges the dominance of things over people through the emancipation of technology from human requirements and human needs through the presentation of achievements whose significance is not primarily humane."[62] For him, the technological prehistory of the phonograph is to be found in mechanical musical instruments like the barrel organ. With these mechanical musical instruments, which now includes the phonograph, "*time* gains a new approach to music."[63] This new approach "is not the time in which music happens, nor is it the time which music monumentalizes by means of its 'style'"; rather it is "time as evanescence, enduring in mute music."[64] "If the 'modernity' of all mechanical instruments gives music an age-old appearance—as if, in the rigidity of its repetitions, it had existed for ever, having been submitted to the pitiless eternity of the clockwork—then the evanescence and recollection that is associated with the barrel organ as a mere sound in a compelling yet indeterminate way has become tangible and manifest through the gramophone records."[65]

9. The phonographic record is a form of writing. The phonographic record, observes Adorno, "is covered with curves, a delicately scribbled, utterly illegible writing."[66] And it is in its connection with writing that Adorno locates the "most profound justification" for the phonographic record in this second essay.

> There is no doubt that, as music is removed by the phonograph record from the realm of live production and from the imperative of artistic creativity and becomes petrified, it absorbs into itself, in this process of petrification, the very life that would otherwise vanish. The dead art rescues the ephemeral and perishing art as the only one alive. Therein may lie the phonograph record's most profound justification, which cannot be impugned by an aesthetic objection to its reification. For this justification reestablishes by the very means of reification an age-old, submerged and yet warranted relationship: that between music and *writing.*[67]

Adorno sees musical notation as an earlier effort to convey music by writing that is limited because notation is only understandable to a limited audience. With the advent of the "writing" of the phonographic record comes Adorno's "hope that . . . it will some day become as readable as the 'last remaining universal language since the construction of the tower.'"[68] Thus, a surprising reversal by Adorno after so much negativity about the record: it holds out the promise of becoming a universal language, which was once merely "conveyed by writing" but now "suddenly itself turns into writing."[69] Writes Adorno, "through the curves of the needle on the phonographic record, music approaches decisively its true character as writing."[70]

OPERA WITHOUT WIGS

The final panel in Adorno's essayistic triptych on the phonograph was published a few months before his death in August 1969. "'Die Oper überwintert auf der Langspielplatte': Theodor W. Adorno über die Revolution der Schallplatte" first appeared in the news magazine *Der Spiegel*.[71] The essay is important because it is largely a retraction of some of Adorno's earlier comments on the phonograph. Hence, it introduces a new albeit late motif regarding the phonographic record.

10. The long-playing record is revolutionary. Adorno says that when he wrote his earlier essays, "it still had to be claimed that, as a form, the phonograph record had not given rise to anything unique to it."[72] In part, this was because when he was writing these essays in the 1920s and early 1930s, there were no long-playing records available. Although the long-playing record was introduced by RCA in 1931, it was only for use in radio, wherein it "provided a means of transcription that allowed material to be prerecorded and exchanged between different stations."[73] It would not be until 1948, long after Adorno's opinions on the phonograph were set, that the 33 1/3 rpm microgroove LP record was launched by Columbia in the United States. Instead of changing the record every three or four minutes as one did with the 78 rpm record about which Adorno had been writing, the 33 1/3 rpm LP allowed for a much longer listening time before having to switch out the record. Particularly in the "classical market," the LP was a rapid success.[74]

The advent of LP records radically changed his opinion of the phonograph record. Adorno now says "the term 'revolution' is hardly an exaggeration with regard to the long-playing record."[75] "The entire musical literature could now become available in quite-authentic form to listeners desirous of auditioning and studying such works at a time convenient to them."[76] Ironically, the technology that changed Adorno's position on the record was introduced to the market for financial reasons, namely, to allow the record industry to better compete with the emerging television industry (just as years earlier the talking movie was introduced in part to better compete with the emerging radio industry).[77]

In particular, this "revolution" is linked to the ability of long-playing records to present operas "[s]horn of phony hoopla," "powdered ladies and gentlemen," and "the Germanic beards in the *Ring*."[78] Long-playing records allow listeners "to recapture some of the force and intensity that had been worn threadbare in the opera houses" through the limitations of staging and costuming. Whether one uses period staging, which in the case of Mozart's *Figaro* "resembles the praline box," or uses "the practices of contemporary dance, dressed in sweat suits or even timeless outfits, one cannot avoid asking, What's the point?"[79] The LP allows one "to spare Mozart [and other operatic composers] from this"—and focus our attention on what is important in opera: the music.

The "short-playing records of yesteryear—acoustic daguerreotypes that are already now hard to play in a way that produces a satisfying sound due to the lack of proper apparatuses—unconsciously also corresponded to their epoch: the desire for highbrow diversion, the salon pieces, favorite arias, and the Neopolitan semi-hits."[80] For Adorno, the advent of the LP record marked a close to "this sphere of music," for "there is now only music of the highest standards and obvious kitsch, with nothing in between."[81] "The LP expresses this historical change rather precisely."[82] Thus, he sees in the development of the phonographic record a pattern not uncommon in the history of music, namely, "it is not all that rare for technological inventions to gain significance only long after their inception."[83]

So, in this late essay, Adorno does a complete 180-degree turn regarding the significance of the phonographic record to music: whereas earlier he viewed it as a flawed musical development of modernity, he later understands it as a welcome technological invention that allows listeners to more perfectly appreciate opera. Still, the LP record is not without its deficiencies. Chief among them are the "rather steep prices" of LP records, "the manipulation of the sound" by the recording engineers, and the making of cuts within an operatic act. Notwithstanding these relatively minor mechanical and economic issues, the LP record "might well be able to help resurrect opera in a decisive way at a time when it has become anachronistic in its own loci."[84] So the distance of phonographic records from the live performance of music becomes a benefit not a limit in the case of opera in the late 1960s. "LPs provide the opportunity—more perfectly than the supposedly live performances—to recreate without disturbance the temporal dimension essential to operas."[85] Thus, circa 1969, the "relevance of the talking machine," one of his earlier motifs, is no longer debatable for Adorno—at least when it comes to the importance of records to operatic music.

CONCLUSION

Adorno's early impressions of the phonograph record were not favorable ones. He saw this technology as an imperfect "trend" that contributed little if nothing to the advancement of music— even though phonograph records held the potential as a form of writing to be become a "universal language." It was only in the last year of his life that he came to recognize a major value for the phonograph record—albeit at the expense of the theatrical elements of opera. Still, there are signs that his transformation in attitude toward the phonographic record was not simply a "death bed conversion" in 1969.

In the winter term of 1961–62, Adorno delivered a series of lectures on music at the Frankfurt School, with parts of them also broadcast over North German Radio. They were published in 1962 under the title *Einleitung in die Musiksoziologie* and later translated into English as *Introduction to the Sociology of Music*. Although this volume only contains a few brief statements about phonographic records, they are significant ones as they provide a good bridge between his early pessimism and later optimism.

Adorno states in the lectures that records give listeners the opportunity through repeated listening to acquaint themselves with and become more educated about music. "In principle, the medium of the record," comments Adorno, "would enable us today to make all of musical literature available to all of those willing to hear, and this potential abolition of educational privilege in music should outweigh the disadvantages which hoarding records as a hobby of an audience of consumers involves under present conditions."[86] Adorno also notes that records "technically have now been vastly perfected, especially since LP recording broke the time barrier that limited older discs to short pieces and often to genre music, excluding the great symphonic forms and making records the musical counterpart of bric-à-brac."[87] Years earlier, he had commented that when we listen "to a recorded symphony the interruptions always remind the listener of the separation between the record and the live performance and destroy the music continuum."[88] This now takes us to possibly the central reason that Adorno had for so long been pessimistic about phonograph records: the music that he preferred was not well represented on vinyl.

The ensuing comments in his *Introduction to the Sociology of*

Music begin to confirm this point. He writes, "Thus the phonographic record, which might accomplish a productive change in musical consciousness, reproduces every dubious side of current judgment. One would need a catalog of what is missing: to this day, for instance, only a small part of Schönberg's oeuvre is accessible in Germany."[89] And, as in the case of another member of the Schoenberg school, even though recordings were available, they might be bad ones: "the first recordings of Berg operas were caricatures bound to reinforce the social prejudice against things modern."[90] This is all complicated further by the difficulties of purchasing quality records in shops that did not normally stock them: "Outside of New York it could quite recently happen that a record shop would refuse to order a serious modern disc because ordering a single one did not pay."[91]

As his work from the 1960s indicates, there is hope for records because their form now allows for the distribution of the kind of music that Adorno prefers: "serious music," or what is called more popularly and crassly "classical music." When Adorno was forming his early thoughts on the phonograph, the technology had not yet caught up with his musical preferences. It simply was either not listenable on the gramophone or not available on record. Yet, when it starts to become available, that is, in the late fifties and early sixties, one can see him start to shift to a more positive attitude toward the phonograph record. Whereas his early work struggled to philosophically understand a key feature of modernity, namely, the ability to write sound, his later works came to find a decisive role for it in society.

Adorno's modernist perceptions of the phonograph record were formed relatively early in his life and its life. The ability to put symphonic music to record was still in its infancy, and the kinds of music that Adorno wanted to hear on record either were not yet available or sounded bad. For him, the phonograph had more in common with the world of the barrel organ and the potter's wheel than that of high fidelity and stereophonic sound. This leads one to wonder, Would he have regarded today's 180-gram vinyl as "canned food"? Would he have viewed the curves of the needle differently if they were tracing the path of a studio recording of his First String Quartet or his opera *Der Schatz des Indianer-Joe*? Adorno on vinyl might have changed everything for this music-obsessed philosopher-composer.[92]

CHAPTER THREE

IT MIGHT GET LOUD

The advent of vinyl was paved by a fifty-year journey that began with a stylus reading a groove on a wax cylinder.[1] Thomas Edison's phonograph, which converts the wax cylinder's grooves into sound via a diaphragm, was developed in 1877. The first sound recording played back on the phonograph was Edison mouthing the words, "Mary had a little lamb."

In one sense, the story of sound recording begins with these words and moves through nearly 150 years of sound recording development from wax cylinders and vinyl records to compact discs and MP3s. The standard tale here is one of increasing levels of sound fidelity—a journey from the low fidelity of the gramophone to the high fidelity of the compact disc. However, in another, more philosophical sense, the invention and development of the phonograph marks a very late stage in the development of sound recording—a journey that dates back to a power first attributed only to the gods.

In this chapter, I would like to explore the general idea that *power comes through the ability to control sound in society* from two different but related directions. The first brings together Theodor W. Adorno's concerns with the phonograph record and Jacques Attali's theses about the role of sound control in social and political power to argue for a unique role for sound control in the neoliberal economy: namely, that the invention of high fidelity plays an important role in sustaining the political economy of music established by Attali. In short, if Adorno is right that the most authentic sound from phonograph records was set before technical advancements in sound quality and control, and Attali is right that what we call the new economy—late capitalism or neoliberalism—grew in strength along with the development of the record industry, then the invention of high fidelity was necessary to ensure that the authenticity issues alluded to by Adorno did not stunt the growth of both the record industry and neoliberalism. The conclusion that follows from this is that the recording studio became, in effect, "the control room" of late capitalism.

The second direction examines Attali's theses about noise control through a reading of Spike Lee's film *Do the Right Thing* (1989). I will argue that Lee's film illustrates how resisting sound control—that is, the control room of late capitalism—has the potential to bring about social and political justice. Lee's film suggests that there is a correlative relationship between sound control and economic control that reveals both the limits of neoliberalism as well as the emancipatory potential of sound.

In sum, if the illusion of high fidelity keeps the neoliberal economy chugging along, then the practice of noise control protects it against failure. Let's begin though by looking back at the divine powers of sound control before respectively passing on to considerations of high fidelity and then noise control.

WAX POWER

The ancient gods were said to have three essential powers: making war, causing famine, and recording sound.[2] This might seem like an odd triumvirate of powers, particularly the latter power, but imagine a world where there is no means to store information other than memory. The sounds that we make to one another in discourse, and those that we hear in the world around us, can only be repeated and passed along to others through acts of memory.

It is somewhat fitting then that when the ancient Greek philosopher Plato discussed memory, he asked us to imagine it in one sense as a "block of wax, which in this or that individual may be larger or smaller, and composed of wax that is comparatively pure or muddy, and harder in some, softer in others, and sometimes just the right consistency."[3] "Let us call it," he says, "the gift of the Muses' mother, Memory, and say that whenever we wish to remember something we see or hear or conceive in our own minds, we hold this wax under the perceptions or ideas and imprint on it as we might stamp the impression of a seal ring. Whatever is so imprinted we remember and know so long as the image remains; whatever is rubbed out or has not succeeded in leaving an impression we have forgotten and do not know."[4] Although the imprinting of perceptions or ideas on wax here has more in common with block printing than a stylus making sound impressions on soft wax, the notion that this act might be regarded as "the gift" of a god to humankind assumes that the actual power of total memory is one held by the gods—and not humankind.

Plato also says that Homer too struggles to explain human memory and "hints at the mind's likeness to wax." He attributes to Homer the view that "When a man has in his mind a good thick slab of wax, smooth and kneaded to the right consistency . . . the impressions that come through the senses are stamped on [the] tables of the 'heart.'"[5] Wax then for thinkers following the leads of Homer and Plato embodies the potential of sound recording—a potential that is ironically or perhaps even fittingly—first fulfilled in the late nineteenth century by Edison by means of the selfsame medium: wax. The implication then that the Muses' mother, Memory, has a mind of perfectly constituted wax that preserves all recorded sound offers one way to understand how recorded sound as memory might be regarded as a godly power in ancient civilizations. But still, set next to the power to create war and cause famine, that is, to take away life, doesn't the biopower of recorded sound pale in comparison? Wars and famines are the instruments of death and destruction in which life is always precarious. The gods have the ability to both give life and take it away, and these powers in the form of inflicting war and famine upon humankind are their most awesome and fear inducing. Given the biopower of war and famine, might we expect outcomes of a similar order to also be attributed to those with the ability to record sound?

First of all, without the ability to record sound it would be very difficult to have any reliable information—that is, "knowledge"—of the past including knowledge of past wars and famines.[6] Indeed, the context of Plato's comments on the waxen nature of memory were part of a more general effort to define knowledge. Recorded sound gives us the ability to know, for example, that the first war in recorded history took place in Mesopotamia in 2700 BCE between Sumer and Elam and that one of the first famines on record occurred from 2770–2730 BCE during the reign of the Egyptian pharaoh Djeser. We also know through recorded sound that this ancient famine was caused by the failure of the Nile to break its banks seven years in a row.[7] Knowledge of these events and others from history are only possible because they have been passed down to us through early sound recording.

However, it is also certain that there were wars caused by humankind before the one that took place in Mesopotamia in 2700 BCE, but because there is no record of them, we have no knowledge of them. Same too with famines, both those caused by natural circumstances such as drought and those "deliberately engineered to kill." In fact, we know through recorded sound that in the ancient Greco-Roman world, "siege-induced famines were not unusual" and that "military manuals explained how to destroy food supplies and poison water reservoirs."[8] These records show, for example, that Julius Caesar used a siege-induced famine to conquer Vercingetorix's Gauls at Alesia in 52 BCE.[9]

Moreover, the line between knowledge of the past and its absence is in large measure marked by the ability to record sound. Therefore, our knowledge of the time before the invention of the cuneiform script, the first writing, in Mesopotamia (which is now called Iraq) in 3200 BCE is very limited. The prehistoric era is thus generally set as ending around the time of the invention of writing, or for our purposes, around the time of the invention of sound recording. And while the oldest known cave paintings are said to be forty thousand years old, and predate by far the invention of sound recording, their power is of a different order than that of early sound recordings. While these prehistoric cave paintings are amazingly beautiful art, they do not provide much more knowledge of the past than fossils and bones excavated from the ground.

The ability then of the gods to record sound is the ability to know the history of the world in its totality—and with this knowledge comes great power. By comparison, the scattered fragments recorded in history books or recounted from generation to generation pale. Recording though is important not just because it provides us with a more extensive knowledge of the past but also because these records can be used as a means of social and political control. In fact, as you will recall from chapter 1, Attali goes so far as to propose "Recording has *always been* a means of social control, a stake in politics, regardless of the available technologies."[10]

"Always," of course, does not mean "forever" but rather refers to the five-thousand-year history of recording. It is a period that extends backward from the digital recording of the present through Edison's invention of sound recording and the recorded histories of ancient Greece and Rome back to the cuneiform script of Mesopotamia. During this period, the period of recording, writes Attali, "Power is no longer content to enact its legitimacy; it records and reproduces the societies it rules. Stockpiling memory, retaining history or time, distributing speech, and manipulating information has always been an attribute of civil and priestly power, beginning with the Tables of the Law."[11] Ancient lore has it too that the necessity and power of recording sound increased as the bond of the verbal contract began to weaken and break down. Recording provided more assurance that contracts and agreements between parties would be honored and thus increased the level of control in society.

Still, the amount of social and political control available through recording was relatively limited compared to what occurred after Edison's invention. Attali comments that "before the industrial age," recording "did not occupy center stage: Moses stuttered and it was Aaron who spoke. But there was already no mistaking: the reality of power belonged to he who was able to reproduce the divine word, not to he who gave it voice on a daily basis."[12] But with Edison's invention and the advances in sound recording that followed, *power came through the ability to control sound in society*. "Possessing the means of recording allows one to monitor noises, to maintain them, and to control their repetition within a determined code," writes Attali. "In the final analysis, it allows one to impose one's own noise and to silence others," he continues. Attali then directly follows this comment with a chilling quote from Adolf Hitler from the *Manual of German Radio* published in 1938: "Without the loudspeaker, we would never have conquered Germany."[13]

Radio though is not a means of sound recording. Still, it is a primary means of sound control and, used appropriately, a vehicle of power, especially in the first half of the twentieth century. Fittingly, the same year as Hitler's remark about the controlling power of radio, Adorno would move from England, where he had been living since fleeing National Socialism in Germany in 1934, to New York City for the purpose of working at the Princeton Radio Research Project.

Although it was not Adorno's aim at the time to either leave

Europe or write extensively on radio, the Princeton Radio Research Project, which provided Adorno with a funded position, gave Max Horkheimer, who set up the opportunity, a way to bring Adorno to New York City. From his arrival in New York City in February of 1938 through November of 1941, when funding for his position was not renewed, Adorno wrote extensively on radio. His major work from this period, *Current of Music: Elements of a Radio Theory*, was left unfinished at his death and has recently been reconstructed and published.[14]

I mention Adorno's work here because in *Current of Music* and elsewhere, he comments on the ways in which sound recording affects music. In *Current of Music*, his express topic is how radio transmission transforms our perception of music. His critical physiognomy of live radio music, while less savage than his critique of phonographic music, is still highly negative of the emancipatory potential for music transmitted by radio. He sees both (and not just phonographic music as noted in the previous chapter) as "steps in the mechanization of musical production,"[15] which he views as destroying authenticity in music. Here again is the key passage from Adorno on the destruction of authenticity in mechanically reproduced music with his added comments about radio: "Now, we believe that *this* authenticity, or aura, is vanishing in music because of mechanical reproduction. The phonograph record destroys the 'now' of the live performance and, in a way, its 'here' as well. Although the ubiquity of radio observes the 'now,' it certainly is more hostile to the 'here.'"[16] In short, for Adorno, music and our perception of it changed in the age of mechanical reproduction, albeit not for the better. Music became both a commodity and an industry through its mechanical reproduction. However, Adorno does not take the social, political, and economic implications of recording sound as far as Attali, who argues that the phonographic record brought about a new economy: neoliberalism.

THE RHETORIC OF HIGH FIDELITY

Prior to 1958, there were no commercially available sound recordings in stereo. But that all changed when the record company Audio Fidelity previewed a "stereo" long-playing recording at the Times Auditorium in New York City on December 13, 1957. On one side of the LP was a stereo recording of the Dukes of Dixieland jazz band and on the other were railroad sound effects from steam and diesel locomotives. The initial print run was five hundred records, and Audio Fidelity offered free copies through an advertisement in *Billboard* magazine to anyone in the music industry who asked for one.

Then, on December 13, 1957, they introduced the first-ever commercial recordings in "stereophonic" two-channel sound. These new stereophonic records though were a luxury as not only did they require special equipment to play them, but they were much more expensive to produce—and therefore to purchase. The company, Audio Fidelity, was known for their "studies in hi fidelity sound," that is, long-playing records that supposedly showcased the high-end sound capabilities of vinyl records. For example, in 1954, they released their debut album in this genre, *Merry Go Round Music*, a collection that the liner notes claimed to be "refreshingly pleasant, particularly for children" though advised to be "[t]aken in reasonably small doses."[17]

But in spite of the increased expense of purchasing and playing these records, stereophonic two-channel sound would by the end of 1958 be made commercially available by every major record label. Yet, at the same time, all of these record labels also released long-playing records in "mono," a two-version record release practice that continued well into the 1960s. There were even "Stereo Demonstration Records" available that high fidelity aficionados could use to test the effectiveness of their stereo playback systems. Decca records, for example, released one in 1958 called "FFSS· Full Frequency Stereophonic Sound."

Often, the two record release system resulted in different cover design and language, catering respectively to their different high fidelity markets. Consider, for example, the Platters 1959 Mercury Records album *Remember When?* Formed in 1952, the Platters were one of the most successful vocal groups of the early rock and roll era with forty singles making the record charts between 1955 and 1967. One of the first African American groups to be accepted as a major chart group, and, for a period of time, the most success-ful vocal group in the world, they were a perfect candidate at the time for a "luxury" recording release. By the time of the release of *Remember When?* the vocal group had already charted twenty singles in the United States alone.

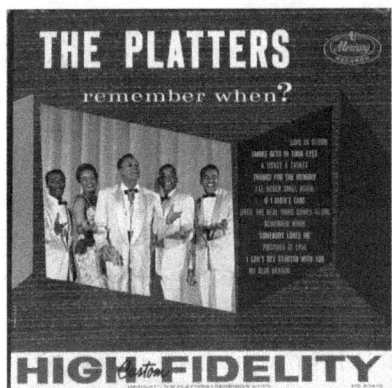

The mono release (MG-20410) of *Remember When?* has a white space at the bottom of the front of the album cover with the words "HIGH FIDELITY" in large red letters with "*Custom*" superimposed in cursive lettering. The back of the album has the same verbiage but much smaller in the lower bottom quarter. The top half of the back is a photo of the group, and the bottom half is divided into half, with the left bottom half listing the songs and right bottom half giving an album description that begins "Here is a package of delicious memories, wrapped, tied, and delivered by the most popular singing group in the world" and ending with the sentence, "These are the songs for catching new memories of today, for mak-ing you pause and say in later years, 'Remember when . . .'" This high fidelity recording then is marketed as yesterday's, today's, and tomorrow's "memories," a perennial vinyl purchase that you will cherish for your lifetime.

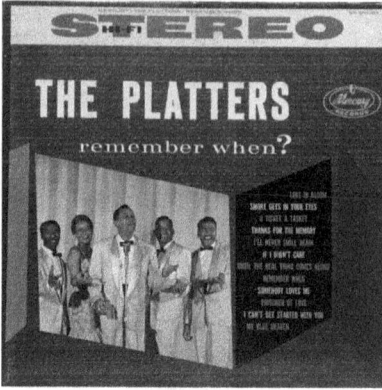

The stereo release (SR-60087) of *Remember When?* has a white space at the top of the front of the album with the word "STEREO" in large purple letters with the words "HI-FI" superimposed in black in a plain font. Like the mono version, the back of the album has the same verbiage but much smaller in the lower bottom quarter. But the similarities with the back covers stop there. First, below the "STEREO/HI-FI" on the back cover is the following printed in very small font size:

> This Mercury STEREO record has been cut with variable groove spacing and electronic groove depth control, thus producing a 2-channel disc of exceptionally wide dynamic range, reliable stylus tracking throughout the frequency range, and startling clarity and definition of instrumental timbres.

> This Mercury STEREO record should be played according to the RIAA standard with a stereo reproducing cartridge having a stylus tip not exceeding .7 mil. For best results, be sure that your two loudspeakers and amplifiers are correctly balanced in terms of output and phase, and that the loudspeakers are placed in the room so as to provide an even "spread of sound" from one to the other.

Second, instead of the back cover content being divided horizontally, it is divided vertically, with the right half cramming in the entire back mono cover text into this space: 1/3 of it for the group photo, 1/3 of it for the song list, and the other 1/3 for the same "delicious" album description. Then, below all of this the "STEREO/HI-FI" icon with above noted "stereo" blurb in small font.

However, it is the left half of the back cover of the stereo version that is completely different than the mono version of the album. Along with a photo of a recording studio, there is the following text:

> This two-track recording was made in Studio A of the Compaigne [sic] Phonographique Francaise, Paris, France. Volume of this studio is 43,000 cubic feet. Reverberation time is 0.65 seconds from the lowest to highest frequencies recorded. Low frequency absorption is obtained from completely floating inside walls covered with small vibrating panels. High frequency absorption is rendered by rockwood pyramids, while sound diffusion, especially characteristic of Studio A, is gained thru wood pyramids.

This general description of the recording studio is then followed by more specific information about some of the sound control technology used in the recording of the record album:

> echo chamber—The echo chamber is really a reverberation chamber which must be added to studio sound. Reverberation time varies from one to three seconds.

> speech imput equipment—Studio A's audio consists of a control panel of 10 line or mike mixers, two echo injections and one general and five independent echo channels. For stereo, the 10 mixers can be split into two times five imputs (for two stereo signals) and then later combined for a monaural signal (via a special combining network in the line amplifier.)

mixing controls—All mixing controls are studio-sliding-contacting-attenuators (Telefunken W 66) Carbon composition type resistors are employed in the W 66 to insure [sic] smooth and noiseless adjustments.

amplifiers—Amplifiers, except for the monitor-power amplifiers, are studio pre-amplifiers V-72 (Siemens). Tiny self-contained units, each has its own individually operated power supply. The two-stage hi-fi amp has a gain of 34 db at extremely low distortion. Used in these sessions as a mike-amp; line amp and even as an isolation amp.

monitoring equipment—The amplifier, a 25 watt V 69 Telefunken is a high power unit with extremely low distortion and flat frequence response. The loud speaker is an Electro-Voice SP 15 with very low transient distortion.

This is all great information about Studio A of the Compagnie Phonographique Française, Paris, France. However, it is followed by some additional "HI-FInformation" about another recording studio:

Recorded stereophonically at Barclay Studios Hoche, Paris, France, the following accent mikes were utilized:

Left Channel Pickup	Right Channel Pickup
bass and guitar—RCA 44BX	24 violins—Neumann U-47
drums—Neumann U-47	8 violas and 4 cellos—Neumann KM-54
piano—RCA 77-DX	3 clarinets—Neumann U-47
harp—Neumann U-47P	1 flute and 1 oboe—Neumann U-47
vocal solo—Neumann U-47	vocal group—Neumann U-47

A pair of Neumann U-47's, set apart and above the grouped musicians and the Platters, recorded the separate left and right stereo channels, augmented by the above accent mikes. Stereo tracks were cut at 15 inches per second on a stereo ampex 300. Gerhard Lehner was the engineer.

David Carroll, Musical Director

This, of course, is a lot of technical information. Obviously, the purchaser of the stereo version of the Platters, *Remember When?* is supposed to be both informed and impressed by it and can use this technical information to justify the higher price of the hi-fi stereophonic two-channel sound recording as compared to the lower priced hi-fi "custom" mono recording. While it is possible, it is not likely that someone would reject this album because of the "accent mike" choices (e.g., Why did they use the U-47P for the harp and not the U-47?). What then is the real purpose of the information on the left back half of this album jacket? Its purpose is to convince the consumer that there are qualitative fidelity gradations in sound recording that merit not only differentiations in the prices of the recordings and the phonographic equipment used to play them but, more generally, that fidelity matters with regard to sound recordings.

Each year the fidelity bar with regard to recorded music goes up incrementally. This is a story regarding the marketing of phonographic records that goes back to its beginnings. Take, for example, a 1908 advertisement for the Victor Talking Machine. The ad, featuring an image of a singing woman opposite an image of the Victor Talking Machine, includes the following text:

Which is which?

You think you can tell the difference between hearing grand-opera artists sing and hearing their beautiful voices on the *Victor*. But can you?

In the opera-house corridor scene in "The Pit" at Ye Liberty Theatre, Oakland, Cal., the famous quartet from Rigoletto was sung by Caruso, Abbot, Homer and Scotti on the *Victor*, and the delighted audience thought they were listening to the singers themselves.

Every day at the Waldorf-Astoria, New York, the grand-opera stars sing, accompanied by the hotel orchestra of sixteen pieces. The diners listen with rapt attention, craning their necks to get a glimpse of the singer. But it is a *Victor.*

In the rotunda of Wanamaker's famous Philadelphia store, the great pipe organ accompanied Melba on the *Victor*, and the people rushed from all directions to see the singer.

Even in the *Victor* laboratory, employes [*sic*] often imagine they are listening to a singer making a record while they really hear the *Victor*

Why not hear the *Victor* for yourself? Any *Victor* dealer will gladly play any *Victor Records* you want to hear.

There is a *Victor* for every purse—$10 to $300.[18]

To get a sense of the purchasing power of $10 in 1908, consider that in 2019 this amounted to $279.72. And $300 in 1908 amounted to $8,391.72 in 2019.[19] The ad is in effect a "Turing Test" for the Victrola: it challenges the listener to tell the difference between a live vocal performance and the recorded playback of one. Presumably, when hearing the quartet from *Rigoletto* in "The Pit" at Ye Liberty Theatre, one will believe that it is being sung live by Caruso, Abbot, Homer, and Scotti when in fact their voices are being played back on a state-of-the-art Victrola.

It has been persuasively argued by Jonathan Sterne that "[p]eople had to learn how to understand the relations between sounds made by people and sounds made by machines."[20] So early advertisements by phonograph companies instructed people how to "understand" sound recordings. Close your eyes, suggested the ads, and try to tell the difference between a live performance and a recorded playback—a tradition in sound recording marketing that has continued at least through the cassette era with memorable ads like "Is it live, or is it Memorex?"

By 1927, the year Adorno would publish the first of his three major essays on the phonograph, Victrolas were now not just tabletop machines with big horns jutting out but elegant pieces of stand-alone furniture. In an ad by the company from this year, one again finds the image of a singing woman but this time set beside an "Orthophonic Victrola," specifically "The Credenza, Model Number Eight-thirty." Whereas the 1908 ad for the Victor plays on the uniqueness and wonder of hearing a "human voice" coming from a machine, twenty years later, the fidelity bar has demonstrably risen, with the language of "high fidelity" sound beginning itself to gel and take shape:

The human voice *is* human on the New Orthophonic Victrola.

A great artist sings in concert, and thousands press for admittance. Many wait in line for hours. Some are turned away, disappointed. Attend the concerts, by all means, but enjoy these same golden voices in your own home . . . whenever you wish . . . through the new Orthophonic Victrola.

This amazing instrument brings you vocal music in all its original purity and power. Tones of correct, natural volume; neither too thin nor too loud, but full, round and mellow. The new Orthophonic Victrola catches the very personality of the artist.

In no other way *can* you have such singing in your home, for the Orthophonic Victrola is based upon Victor's new, scientific, Victor-controlled principle—"matched impedance."

Another Victor achievement equaling that of the Orthophonic instrument, is the new Orthophonic Victor Record. It has new beauty and depth, a richer resonance. Recorded by microphone, and made from an improved material, practically all foreign noises have been eliminated. The new Victor Records are living re-creations of the artists themselves.

Words can give you but the faintest impression of the thrill in store for you at the nearest Victor dealer's. Have a demonstration today. Go . . . in your most skeptical mood! There are many beautiful models of the Orthophonic Victrola, from $95 to $300, list price. Silent electric motor ($35 extra) eliminates winding. You play . . . and relax.[21]

The road from this 1927 ad with its rhetoric of recording tonality (e.g., "tones" can be thick or thin, empty or full, soft or loud, harsh or mellow, and so on) to the rhetoric of the 1959 Platters' album sound control room is just a thirty-year journey, and the Platters' album is only fifty years removed from marketing efforts just trying to explain what a "talking machine" does, namely, reproduce the human voice.

When Adorno wrote his first analysis of the phonographic record in 1927, he too was caught up in the mechanistic dimensions of the sound recording. However, unlike Victor and the other gramophone companies who were trying to get customers and listeners to see beyond the oddity of reproducing sound mechanically, Adorno saw all efforts at "mechanical music" including radio broadcasts, phonographic records, and film scores for both silent and sound film as mere "trends" and, in the case of phonographic records, trends that he was not "buying." He regarded "talking

machines" with their "mahogany cabinets on little rococo legs"[22] to be status symbols of debatable relevance to music. Comparable in his estimation to the photograph, the more phonographic records attempt to control sound, the more phonographically recorded sounds become inauthentic. Again, it is important here to recall that for Adorno, whereas the early photographic technology "had the power to penetrate rationally the reigning artistic practice," later efforts that claimed higher fidelity were merely a technological "illusion."[23] Moreover, as noted earlier, the same technological illusion holds for the phonograph.

For Adorno, the more music "recordings become more perfect in terms of plasticity and volume," the more "the subtlety of color and the authenticity of vocal sound declines as if the singer were being distanced more and more from the apparatus."[24] In short, as technology works to improve sound fidelity, sound authenticity declines proportionally. This again is established in the fascinating fact that Adorno was not interested in accounting for the changes in sound recording technology over the forty-year span of the republication of his essay "Nadelkurven" in 1965 because he believed that it only further confirmed what he wrote in 1927: that is, *records have been on the decline ever since the invention of the "talking machine."* Not even the new commercial recordings in stereophonic two-channel sound produced with low-frequency absorption obtained from completely floating inside walls covered with small vibrating panels and high-frequency absorption rendered by rockwood pyramids could shake this conviction.

I point out Adorno's position on the phonographic record here for several reasons. First, it is very clear from at least as early as the late 1920s that Adorno rejected the idea that the fidelity of records could be improved with technological development. In fact, he considered it to be an illusion, one which he from a very early point in his career links to efforts by the recording industry not only to get people to buy phonographs and phonographic records but to draw them away from live musical performances, the space of authentic musical reproduction. And while the early ads from Victor like the one from 1927 noted above encourage consumers of music to "Attend the concerts, by all means," they also suggest to avoid waiting "in line for hours" and "enjoy these same golden voices in your own home . . . whenever you wish."

Second, throughout his career, one that spanned the early

development of the talking machine through the invention of stereophonic sound and the long-playing record, Adorno consistently rejected not only the technology of sound recording but also its products. Although in his last year he found opera records to be useful, it was not for the reasons given by the industry, such as to avoid waiting "in line for hours." Rather, he found these records useful only because he saw the live performance of opera to be in decline and found that because opera records allowed you to listen to the music without having to endure its "theatrical" aspects, there was some value in operatic recordings circa 1968—as a way to save operatic music.

From a very young age, Adorno saw through the invention of high and higher fidelity as the technological perfection of musical recording. He saw it for what it is and was, namely, a commercial effort by the record and recording industry to get consumers to learn how to understand the relations between "sounds made by people and sounds made by machines." The major aim of such efforts was not philosophical edification but rather economic enterprise, that is, to get consumers to purchase recorded sound. This marketing ruse extends to the quasi-philosophical notion that recorded sound somehow "embeds" the original sound in the recording.

As Sterne explains, "reproduced sounds are not simply mediated versions of unmediated originals."[25] "Sound reproduction is a social process," where "[t]he possibility of reproduction precedes the fact."[26] Sound fidelity was invented through sound control in the recording studio. Writes Sterne,

> Sound fidelity is much more about faith in the social function and organization of machines than it is about the relation of a sound to its "source." . . . From the very beginning, sound reproduction was a studio art, and, therefore, the source was as bound up in the social relations of reproducibility as any copy was. Sound fidelity is a story that we tell ourselves to staple separate pieces of sonic

reality together. The efficacy of sound reproduction as a technology or as a cultural practice is not in its keeping faith with a world wholly external to itself. On the contrary, sound reproduction— from its very beginnings—always implied social relations among people, machines, practices, and sounds. The very concept of sound fidelity is a result of this conceptual and practical labor.[27]

Moreover, efforts to help us to connect "mechanical music" with "live" music go to the very use of the term *live* with reference to music. As Sarah Thornton has pointed out, the term *live* with connection to music only entered the music appreciation lexicon in the 1950s, where it was "part of a public relations campaign by musician's unions in Britain and the United States."[28] At the time of the campaign, "the word *live* was short for *living*, as in *living musicians*."[29] However, writes Thornton, "[l]ater, it referred to music itself and quickly accumulated connotations which took it beyond the denotative meaning of performance . . . Through a series of condensations . . . the expression 'live music' gave positive valuation to and became generic for performed music. It soaked up the aesthetic and ethical connotations of life-versus-death, human-versus-mechanical, creative-versus-imitative."[30] If the phonographic record struggled in its early history to make a connection to humans, both their voices and their lives, then by the 1950s this was solved by transferring the "life" of "living musicians" to the musical recording itself. In the process, it is the musical recording that comes to have the attributes of life through the term *live* used in relationship to it.

The biopolitics of this transfer cannot be more obvious: by transferring "living" away from the musicians to mechanical music via the phonographic records, sound control can also be said to "deny life" to musicians and to transfer it onto sound recordings. In doing so, we can add to Attali's idea that "the stockpiling of use-time in the commodity object is fundamentally a herald of death," particularly with regard to vinyl records, another layer of death to vinyl, that of "living musicians" now becoming "living sound" or "live sound," which of course heralds the death of the musician in recorded music.

As Sterne notes, the application of the term *fidelity* to sound was contemporaneous with the invention of the phonograph. Prior to 1877, fidelity was not applied to sound namely because there was no such thing as sound recording in which the human voice could be captured through what Adorno termed *sound writing*. "Fidelity," writes Sterne, "is the quality of faithfulness to some kind of pact or agreement," a notion, noted earlier, that takes us back to the origins of sound recording being born out of the failure of humankind to honor verbal agreements. For Sterne, "the term *sound fidelity* has become a kind of technicistic shorthand for addressing the problems of sound's reproducibility—a gold standard for originals and copies, an imagined basis for the currency in sounds."[31] To this, I would add that the term *high fidelity* has become a kind of shorthand too, although of a different order.

If sound fidelity refers more to the philosophical problems at the heart of sound recording, then high fidelity refers to the control rooms where these philosophical problems become economic ones. For it is in the sound control room that the illusions of fidelity are worked out by engineers who convince the listening masses to consume increasingly perfect sound products. It is not just that the standard of fidelity with regard to sound changes or increases over time; rather, it is the fact that this changing standard is the control room for the neoliberal economy borne out of Attali's age of repetition. It is an economy that is established through a complex network of relations between recording practices, products, and technologies. Although music plays a role in this economy, it has become secondary to the processes that determine its conditions of recording and level of fidelity.

Adorno recognized very early on that fidelity with regard to sound was an invention and marketing ploy of the record industry. Although his approach to emerging generations of sound recording "development" may seem reactionary, particularly his rejection of the latest versions of the Victrola and its recordings, it may in retrospect be viewed as a very early rejection of the emerging economy of late capitalism, particularly if viewed through the lens of Attali's commentary on the political economy of music. The notion of high fidelity keeps music consumers hungry for increasingly higher levels of fidelity in sound recording and reproduction. An entire lexicon is created with regard to levels of tone and types of sound to keep the engine of neoliberalism well fueled and chugging along.

Michel Chion, one of leading theoreticians of sound, has even created a vocabulary to describe the "seven effects enabled by machines" regarding sound, which in his parlance, music is just one aspect. They are capture, telephony, systemic acousmatization, phonofixation, phonogeneration, and reshaping.[32] While each of these seven technological effects has the ability to create sound, "it remains to be seen whether this represents an increase in 'fidelity'—a notion ideologically and aesthetically as risky as would be the notion of faithfulness in the photographic image to the visible of which it provides us with a representation."[33] "In reality," writes Chion, "the term 'high fidelity' is taken up from the rhetoric of advertising."[34] Then, to further his dismissal of the term, he notes that there are "innumerable" differences between the original reverberation and the recorded reverberation including the level of "spectral equilibrium, of space, of texture, and of dynamics."[35]

In my estimation, Chion's work is the knockout blow to the notion that high fidelity means anything more than "buy this record because it keeps the neoliberal economy alive and well." So, arguably, without the notion of high fidelity, the neoliberal sound economy would have melted away like the wax on Edison's cylinders when exposed to high heat. What is most painful about our 130-odd year journey through the amazing world of higher fidelity is the irony that in its late stages, when we thought we were moving beyond vinyl records to compact discs and MP3s because of their higher fidelity and the way they eliminate "noise" such as the pops and crackles heard on all vinyl records, the alleged higher fidelity of these records led to their resurgence today. And, with it, as I have argued previously, give neoliberalism a second life.

NOISE CONTROL

As noted in chapter 1, the evolution of musico-social relations moves through four stages for Attali. In premodern society, the first stage, music is an accompaniment to ritual sacrifice. Its social function is "to make people forget—to make them forget the violence entailed in the structuring differences to found and maintain the social order."[36] Attali is drawing music here into dialogue with work like René Girard's *La Violence et le sacré*,[37] which proposes "a theory of ritual sacrifice as the central act of a cultural system generated by primal violence."[38] In early modern society, the second stage, the function of music is "to make them believe—to make them believe in the intrinsic harmony of the social order under the command of a leader."[39] In the third stage, capitalist society, the function of music is to silence people, "to make them listen silently and endlessly to music designed to distract their attention or stimulate their appetites."[40] In this stage, music has been commodified, with its most uniquely identifiable forms to be found in the "hit parade," Muzak, and the record industry in general. It is only in the fourth stage, post-capitalism, where Attali finds any relief from the musico-social relations associated with the forgetting, believing, and silencing of the earlier stages.

Attali's fourth stage, which he calls *composition*, detaches itself from the technologies of sound recording that were so important to the development of his third stage, which he calls *repetition*. These technologies of sound recording include phonographic records, reel-to-reel tapes, eight-track tapes, cassettes, compact discs, minidiscs, MP3s, and so on. If the emphasis in the age of repetition was the reproduction of sound through recordings, then the emphasis in the age of composition will be live performances, the invention of new musical instruments, and the discovery of new genres of music and codes. As Eugene Holland puts it,

> composition involves the reappropriation of music by ordinary people, and a novel merging of the roles of producer and consumer: rather than slavishly reproduce other people's music from a score, or passively listen to reproductions in silence, people in the era of composition will themselves enjoy their own music. The era of composition will thus put an end to the social alienation of music, which Attali defines as performing in accordance with a programme or code established in advance and by someone else; instead, message and code are to be invented and performed simultaneously in a process of continual creation where the process itself counts for more than the finished product.[41]

For Holland, jazz improvisation bears a strong resemblance to Attali's composition—and I do not disagree with him here. However, not only is the history of jazz improvisation more or less contemporaneous with the development of sound recording, which would fit jazz improvisation into the previous era, namely that of repetition, but in spite of finding its best work in spontaneous live performance, it is not a new genre of music nor does it rely much on the invention of new instruments. In fact, for many jazz purists, new instruments are an anathema to jazz music, and new genres such as jazz fusion are often viewed with disdain.

What I would like to suggest though is that we view moving beyond the age of repetition—and its attendant economy—to be less about the kind of music that is produced and type of instruments used than about the uses of "sound control" in its live performance. Attali is often criticized for leaving his thoughts on the age of composition incomplete, but this can also be viewed as an opportunity to imagine a relationship between music and political economy that moves beyond the neoliberal model found in the age of repetition. To this end, I propose that we view Spike Lee's film *Do the Right Thing* as an effort to challenge the neoliberal economy through its use of music. Namely, the film is an effort to "fight the power" of neoliberalism and racism by breaking the musical silence of capitalism by blasting a hip-hop song throughout the neighborhood.

If it can be said that Hitler could not have conquered Germany without a loudspeaker, then it might in related fashion be said that Radio Raheem (Bill Nunn) attempted to conquer the Bedford-Stuyvesant neighborhood of Brooklyn with only a boom box. The former was the epitome of hatred, evil, and racism, whereas the latter aimed to fight against them—though murdered in the process by the police with the "infamous Michael Stewart choke hold."[42] Mookie (Spike Lee) responds to his murder by calmly walking through the crowd with a garbage can that he has just emptied and throwing it through the plate glass window of Sal's Famous Pizzeria. The angry mob then trashes the pizzeria and sets it on fire. Spike Lee's *Do the Right Thing* is a day in the life of racially troubled America that begins in a radio station control booth and ends with the murder of a young man who set off a race riot by playing his boom box too loud that day. Although sound control is not the theme of the film, it plays an important role in it.

Throughout the film, Radio Raheem walks around the neighborhood with a massive boom box powered by twenty "D" batteries, which we know because of the scene in which he buys them at a convenience store. The volume on his boom box was getting softer, and the cassette tape of Public Enemy's "Fight the Power" was beginning to drag.[43] The Korean clerk misunderstands his request and keeps asking him if he wants "C" batteries. Raheem calls him a "dumb motherfucker" and tells him to "Learn how to speak English first."[44] This though is just a taste of the racial tension set in motion by the use of his boom box.

The first is his sound standoff with a group of Puerto Rican youths. The youths are hanging out on a stoop drinking beer and playing dominoes while salsa music blasts from one of their cars. Radio Raheem approaches them playing as usual his rap music, which is drowned out because of the louder volume of their salsa music. In Spike Lee's script, he notes "Radio Raheem does not like to be bested; the salsa music from the parked car is giving him competition, this is no good."[45] So, in response to their loud salsa music, he turns his rap music to a higher decibel level. The youths then start to yell at him in Spanish but eventually concede to the superiority of his decibel level by turning off the salsa music in their car. Overjoyed that he has won this sound standoff, Raheem smiles and nods to them. He then turns down his volume to what Lee calls a "reasonable listening level"[46] and continues his music bop around the neighborhood. One of the youths, Stevie (Luis Ramos), says to Raheem in admiration and bewilderment, "You got it, bro," and after the competing boom box is out of listening range, he turns back on the salsa music on the car radio.

But the sound standoff with the Puerto Rican youths is merely a prelude to the major sound control battle in the film, namely the one between Sal and Radio Raheem. It begins in the film when Radio Raheem enters Sal's Famous Pizzeria blasting his music asking Sal (Danny Aiello) for "two slices." "No service till you turn dat shit off," responds Sal. "Two slices," replies Radio Raheem. Pino (John Turturro), Sal's son, then echoes his father's request, "Turn it off." Sal then says, "Mister Radio Raheem, I can't even hear myself think. You are disturbing me and you are disturbing my customers."[47] He then reaches under the pizza counter for his Mickey Mantle bat. Everyone in the pizzeria is poised for the moment to explode into violence, but it doesn't this time. Radio Raheem turns off his music at the sight of the bat and continues with his order, "Two slices, extra cheese." Sal puts the bat away and replies, "When you come into Sal's Famous Pizzeria, no music. No rap, no music. Capisce? Understand? . . . This is a place of business. Extra cheese is two dollars."[48]

In the scene before he goes back to pizzeria, where he will be murdered by the police, Radio Raheem runs into another character, Buggin' Out (Giancarlo Esposito), on the street. Buggin' is upset that even though Sal "makes all his money off us Black people," there are only pictures of Italians, "Sylvester Stallone and motherfuckers," on the walls. "We shouldn't buy a single slice, spend a single penny in that motherfucker," says Buggin' Out, "till some people of color are put in there."[49] Buggin' asks Radio why he only plays Public Enemy: "Is that the only tape you got?"[50] "I don't like anything else," replies Radio.[51]

When he enters the pizzeria with Buggin' Out for the last time in the next scene, Radio is playing Public Enemy on his boom box louder than any other time in the film, including the salsa music standoff. Hearing the loud music, Sal says to him, "What did I tell ya 'bout dat noise?" Buggin' Out then rides Sal about there being no black people on the walls of the pizzeria, but Sal ignores him focusing on controlling the "noise" Radio Raheem has brought into his restaurant. "What da fuck!" he says. "Are you deaf?"[52] It then goes downhill quickly from here:

Buggin' Out
No, are you? We want some Black people up on the Wall of
   Fame.

Sal
Turn that JUNGLE MUSIC off. We aint in Africa.

Buggin' Out
Why it gotta be about jungle music and Africa?

Sal
It's about turning that shit off and getting the fuck outta my
   pizzeria.

Pino
Radio Raheem.

Radio Raheem
Fuck you.

Sal
What ever happened to nice music with words you can
   understand?

Radio Raheem
This is music. My music.

Vito
We're closed.

Buggin' Out
You're closed alright, till you get some Black people up on that
   wall.[53]

Sal then loses his temper and grabs his Mickey Mantle bat from
underneath the counter and uses it to destroy Radio Raheem's boom
box, which was sitting on the counter blaring music throughout the
verbal altercation. After a moment of general and musical silence
after the destruction of the boom box, as described in the script
notes of Lee, "Radio Raheem picks Sal up from behind the counter
and starts to choke his ass. Radio Raheem's prized possession—his
box, the thing he owned of value—his box, the one thing that gave
him any sense of worth—has been smashed to bits. (Radio Raheem,
like many Black youth, is the victim of materialism and a misplaced
sense of values.) Now he doesn't give a fuck anymore. He's gonna
make Sal pay with his life."[54] Originally it was planned that "Raheem
would grab Sal by the neck; slam his face into the counter, and drag
him the length of the counter," per Lee in his production notes.[55] But
Danny Aiello, who played Sal in the film, objected that it was too
"slapstick and had been done a million times," so it was decided he
would pull him over the counter rather than give him a "facial."[56]

Either way, Raheem has had it with Sal exercising his power over him by telling him to silence "dat noise." He retaliates by choking Sal in an effort to silence him.

As a counterpoint to Radio Raheem walking around the neighborhood blasting his cassette tape of Public Enemy in his boom box, a radio voice is heard throughout the film. In a journal entry on the film, Lee writes,

> Throughout the film we hear a DJ's voice over the radio, broadcasting from some fictional station. This device has been used to death, but we might be able to rework it.
>
> The station's call name is WE LOVE RADIO. It broadcasts from a storefront on the block. The DJ looks directly out onto the street and observes all the comings and goings. Passersby can watch him as he rocks the mike. This is gonna be very stylized.
>
> The DJ's name is Mister Señor Love Daddy, the world's only 7-24-365 DJ. That's 7 days a week, 24 hours a day, 365 days a year. He never goes to sleep. "I work overtime for your love," he says.
>
> Playing on the final words of *School Daze*, "Please wake up," the first words of *Do the Right Thing* could be the DJ's: "Hello Nueva York. It's time to wake up. It's gonna be hot as a motherfucker." Vicious.[57]

In the film, Lee decides to reduce the workload of this DJ from twenty-four hours a day to twelve hours, making Mister Señor Love Daddy (Samuel Jackson) the "world's only twelve-hour strongman."[58] The first words in the film are indeed, "Waaaake up! Wake up! Wake up! Wake up! Up ya wake! Up ya wake! Up ya wake!"[59] They are being shouted by the DJ into a microphone, but we don't see this. "WE SEE only big white teeth and very Negroidal (*big*) lips," writes Lee in the script. [60] After this, the camera rolls back so that we now see it is a DJ in a radio station mouthing these words. After a bit more radio banter, the camera pushes back further. Writes Lee in the script, "The CAMERA, which is STILL

PULLING BACK, shows that Mister Señor Love Daddy is actually sitting in a storefront window. The control booth looks directly out onto the street. This is WE LOVE RADIO, a modest station with a loyal following, right in the heart of the neighborhood."[61] From his control booth, throughout the film, Mister Señor Love Daddy airs updates and commentary on what is happening in the neighborhood. Everyone who walks by the station can see him twelve hours a day in the control booth and, of course, can hear his voice on the radio by tuning into 108 FM: "The last on your dial, but the first in ya hearts, and that's the truth, Ruth!"[62] "I'se play only da platters dat matter, da matters dat platter and That's the truth Ruth."[63]

Released in the United States on June 30, 1989, *Do the Right Thing* is a masterful commentary on race relations in America at the time. Roger Ebert gives the film his highest praise, saying "I have been given only a few filmgoing experiences in my life to equal the first time I saw *Do the Right Thing*. Only a few penetrate your soul." After viewing it for the first time at the Cannes Film Festival in May of 1989, Ebert walked out thinking "Spike Lee had done an almost impossible thing. He'd made a movie about race relations in America that empathized with all the participants. He didn't draw lines or take sides but simply looked with sadness at one racial flashpoint that stood for many others." Also, for Ebert, "there are really no heroes or villains in the film," although many would disagree with this comment as well as the one that Lee does not "take sides" in the film. Lee has often been asked whether Mookie did the right thing by throwing the garbage can through Sal's window after the murder of Raheem by the police. However, he notes, "Not one person of color has ever asked me that question."[64]

Regardless of whether the film was too middle class versus too militant, or whether Mookie did the right thing, Attali's theory of musico-social relations gives us a powerful theoretical perspective from which to consider the film. If the function of music under capitalism is to silence people, then the actions of Radio Raheem point in the opposite direction. Namely, his journey through the neighborhood blasting a song from Public Enemy allows him to defy the silence of music under late capitalism.

While it is true that he is playing a cassette tape recording that was produced and distributed through one of the corridors of the music industry, it is also true that his journey through the neighborhood playing this song is not a passive act of listening. The changing volume levels of the song are determined by the power struggles he faces at different points in the film. The loudest live performance of the song is left for his confrontation with Sal, who is viewed by Radio Raheem and Buggin' Out as taking financial advantage of the majority African American population of the neighborhood. They point out that Sal is happy to sell them pizza but does not want to celebrate their culture and heritage on the walls of his business. The loud hip-hop music is in effect a live performance of defiance against neoliberalism, and efforts to enact sound control over it are efforts to preserve the neoliberal economy of repetition.

The song itself, "Fight the Power," incorporates various samples and allusions to African American culture, including civil rights exhortations, black church services, and the music of James Brown. Moreover, when Spike Lee asked Public Enemy to compose a song for the film about racial tension in Brooklyn, he "wanted it to be defiant, I wanted it to be angry, I wanted it to be very rhythmic."[65]

But recall in Attali's political economy of music, under both the ages of repetition and composition, music's power does not come from its lyrics. In fact, it has its power in spite of its lyrics. Again, for Attali, the political role of music is not found in "what it conveys, in its melodies or discourses," "but in its very existence."[66] It is important here to recall again what Attali said earlier about the nature of power in the political economy of music in a passage that goes the heart of his biopolitics: "Power in its invading, deafening presence, can be calm: people no longer talk to one another. They speak neither of themselves nor of power. They hear the noises of the commodities into which their imaginary is collectively channeled, where their dreams of sociality and need for transcendence dwell. The musical ideal then almost becomes an ideal of health: quality, purity, the elimination of noises; silencing drives, deodorizing the body, emptying it of its needs, and reducing it to silence."[67] Attali is more concerned about the effect of listening to music than its content. The effect of "Fight the Power" in the film is not passive response but just the opposite: everyone who hears the live performance of the music has a reaction to it. Even the three old, black guys in the film who sit on the corner and talk have a reaction to it; namely, the music is being played too loud. In short, the various efforts to control the sound levels of Radio Raheem's music represent various efforts to confront neoliberalism. Radio Raheem has reappropriated music in support of something beyond neoliberal culture. The radio station in the neighborhood serves as a reminder of the 24-hour, 365-day a week droning of capitalism from its own "control booth." In their failure, Radio Raheem's attempts to break this cycle are both emancipatory and liberating.

CONCLUSION

This chapter began with the attribution of godly power to sound recording and ends with a human-all-too-human youth, Radio Raheem, using sound recording to fight political and economic power. Whereas the history of sound recording reveals its power to give life and to take it away through the manipulation of information and knowledge, and sound control allows one to impose one's noise on others as well as to silence them, the live performance of music offers a way beyond the political and economic implications of noise control. But, like sound recording, noise control is both connected to godly powers and has a long history of social and political use in the exercise of power.

In *The Epic of Gilgamesh*, circa 3000 BCE, the gods were said to use their powers in the exercise of noise control: "In those days the world teemed, the people multiplied, the world bellowed like a wild bull, and the great god was aroused by the clamour. Enlil heard the clamour and he said to the gods in council, 'The uproar of mankind is intolerable and sleep is no longer possible by reason of the babel.' So the gods in their hearts were moved to let loose the deluge."[68] The Romans were the first to enact by-laws in support of noise control. In 44 BCE, Julius Caesar passed the following: "Hence-forward, no wheeled vehicles whatsoever will be allowed within the precincts of the city, from sunrise until the hour before dusk . . . Those which shall have entered during the night, and are still within the city at dawn, must halt and stand empty until the appointed hour."[69] In fact, most cities around the world exercise one form or another of noise control. For example, the city of Bern, Switzerland, has noise control legislation dating back to 1628, when it passed a by-law "[a]gainst singing and shouting in the streets on festival days." Over the years there were many other by-laws including a number prohibiting music playing and music-making, such as an 1879 by-law "[a]gainst the playing of music after 10:30 p.m." and the 1918 by-law "[a]gainst carpet-beating and music-making."[70]

Set alongside the long history of sound control, the control of sound in *Do the Right Thing* can be put in historical context. But to posit Radio Raheem, a youth with a boom box who walks the streets of Brooklyn blasting it, as a prophet of post-capitalism only makes sense in view of Attali's theses on noise control. Otherwise, he is just a young man who wants recognition in a neighborhood where race relations are always already a lit match in a fireworks factory. Still, the power of Lee's highly stereotyped racial imagery provides a strong setting to stage a post-capitalist world awakening from the silencing powers of noise control.

If the age of repetition started with the words "Mary had a little lamb," then the age of composition arguably begins with live performances that fight the power of sound control. Historically speaking though they can easily be stamped out with noise control by-laws, and herein lies the rub of sound control. On the one hand, the biopolitics of the age of repetition are such that stockpiling death through vinyl begets a silence that can only be broken by live performance; on the other hand, although live performance in the age of composition breaks this silence and is life-affirming, it is only possible in a social and political setting free of the legislation of sound, which given its long history does not leave much room for hope—or a post-capitalist utopia.

After all, Radio Raheem is murdered for his efforts to challenge the legislation of sound, whereas Mister Señor Love Daddy continues to thrive in his control room. If Radio Raheem exemplifies the emancipatory powers of music in the age of composition, then Mister Señor Love Daddy might be seen as representing the controlling power of music in the age of repetition. From his control room, he observes and comments on the comings and goings of the neighborhood. Although he implores us to "wake up!" he is more a symbol of the endless droning noise of capitalism that in the end only brings about silence rather than the voice of emancipation. As he says, his 108 FM is "[t]he last on your dial, but the first in ya hearts, and that's the truth, Ruth!"[71] It is a truth that is written on the hearts of the members of the neighborhood like the truth stamped on the heart of Homer's man with a mind composed of "a good thick slab of wax." It is the truth of late capitalism. And, Mister Señor Love Daddy's statement, "I'se play only da platters dat matter, da matters dat platter and That's the truth Ruth,"[72] might be taken as an anthem for vinyl in age of repetition. His "platters dat matter" are not the vocal group but the vinyl records that keep the neoliberal economy chugging along—the only "platters dat matter."

Lee's film only suggests one way it might get loud in a post-capitalist age of live performance. Another way is imagining more music in the streets and squares of America: spontaneous live performances that take music from the silence of headphones to the noise of speakers blaring in celebration of freedom from the powers of noise control. Question is, Will they too be cut down through sound control like Radio Raheem—or will they be allowed to perform their music in the streets and challenge the power that comes through the ability to control sound in society?

Adorno's concerns with the phonograph record and Attali's theses about the role of sound control in social and political power were shown to provide the setting for a unique role for sound control in the neoliberal economy: namely, the invention of high fidelity as a means of sustaining the political economy of music, as established by Attali. If Attali is right that what we call the new economy—late capitalism or neoliberalism—grew in strength along with the development of the record industry, then the invention of high fidelity was necessary to ensure that the authenticity issues alluded to by Adorno did not stunt the growth of both the record industry and neoliberalism. As we saw, the recording studio became, in effect, the control room of neoliberalism. Although Lee's film shows how resisting sound control—that is, the control room—has the potential to bring about social and political justice, because there is a correlative relationship between sound control and economic control, the emancipatory potential of sound is limited. In conclusion, if the illusion of high fidelity perpetuates the neoliberal economy, then the continuing practice of noise control protects it against failure. Only when it becomes loud will we have a definitive sign that the neoliberal economy is in decline.

CHAPTER FOUR

SELLING OUT

On December 16, 1967, the British rock and roll band the Who released one of the strangest albums ever recorded. That same year, the French intellectual Jacques Derrida published a trio of philosophy books that were equally strange in their own way.

The album was "a critique of the forces of commerce that had created and sustained the whole pop industry of the 1950s and 1960s,"[1] while the books were likewise a critique, albeit of the forces of metaphysics that had created and sustained the whole philosophy industry since Greek antiquity. The Who entitled their album *The Who Sell Out*, whereas Derrida avoided the similar but fitting title *Derrida Sells Out Western Philosophy, Volumes 1–3* and went with the more academic titles of *Of Grammatology*, *Speech and Phenomena*, and *Writing and Difference*.

In one way, rock music and Western philosophy were never the same after the Who and Derrida "sold out" their respective enterprises. The Who's album became part of a rising chorus of voices warning about the limits of capitalism and a consumer society and foreshadowed the forces that led to the breakdown of the music and recording industries in the late twentieth and early twenty-first centuries. Likewise, Derrida's early "deconstruction" of metaphysics played a key role in the rise of the linguistic turn in theory that is now in its second generation and has yielded many theoretical alternatives to structuralism and post-structuralism, such as cultural studies, globalization studies, feminism, race and gender studies, queer theory, postcolonialism, Marxism, and new historicism in the late twentieth century as well as a very long list of "studies," such as debt studies, sound studies, surveillance studies, and so on, along with new materialism, object-oriented ontology, and surface reading in the early twenty-first century.

In this chapter, I'd like to argue that there are two fundamentally different ways to "sell out" theory (and music). The first resembles more the work of the Who and Derrida wherein the masterly deployment of critique yields a new type of relationship to their respective industries. It is a relationship that not only demystifies and undermines the extant conditions of the industry but also offers it a different direction. This type of sell out establishes the bar for new directions in music and theory. It is a form of musical and theoretical sell out that is innovative, progressive, and sometimes even strange.

The other way to sell out theory (and music) is to treat it primarily or solely as a means to personal, professional, or financial gain. It involves "using" theory to advance one's career prospects or to gain notoriety or to sell books. The Mothers of Invention featuring Frank Zappa recorded an album from March through October 1967 whose title captures this type of selling out of theory well; *We're Only in It for the Money* was released on March 4, 1968.[2] It was part of a larger project called *No Commercial Potential.*[3] After the Beatles released *Sgt. Pepper's Lonely Hearts Club Band* on May 26, 1967 in the United Kingdom, Zappa changed the album title to parody the Fab Four because he felt that they were insincere and "only in it for the money."[4] He targeted the Beatles as a symbol of the corporatization of youth culture and regarded the album as a criticism of the band in particular and psychedelic rock as a whole.[5]

Front cover of Frank Zappa's
We're Only in It for the Money,
Verve Records (1968).

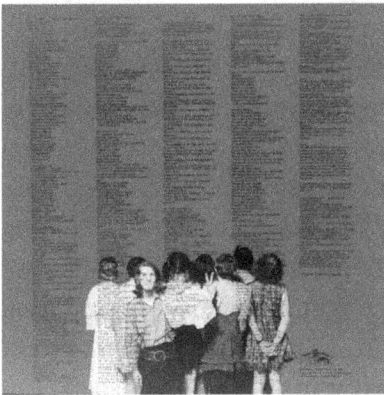

Gatefold of Frank Zappa's *We're Only in It for the Money,* Verve Records (1968).

I'll begin by discussing the Who's recording and state why I believe that its type of sell out is one fundamental way to regard selling out theory. I'll then move on to discuss another way of selling out theory through examples from the work of two contemporary theorists: Terry Eagleton and Rita Felski. The chapter will conclude that it is difficult if not impossible to engage in theory today without implicating oneself in one or both of these sell outs. Nevertheless, each way has radically different implications for the theory industry and its institutions.

THE WHO GET ON TRACK

The Who were well known for defying the norms of the 1960s pop scene. If the Beatles and the Rolling Stones set those norms, then the Who broke them. From the guitar and drum smashing of their early live performances to the group's angry, defiant, and aggressive songs, the Who embodied musical nihilism like no other rock and roll band in the 1960s. And no song set this tone for the Who like their early hit single "My Generation," which has been aptly described as "the Who's statement of noise as art—their manifesto of ear-jarring chaos that connected so directly with dissident youth consciousness of the times."[6]

Their managers were two ex-film industry mavericks, Kit Lambert and Chris Stamp, who just happened to stumble upon them at the Harrow and Wealdstone Railway Hotel in 1964. Lambert and Stamp were looking for a subject for a feature film and stopped their search after hearing the band. And although Lambert and Stamp wanted to make a film, as did the group, a company willing to put up the funds could not be found. The Who would have to wait until 1975 to have a feature film. The film, *Tommy*, was vastly different from the one envisioned in their early years by their managers.

To say that the Who rejected the commercial aspects of the music industry of the 1960s is only partly true. It is also the case that aspects of the entertainment industry of the time rejected them. For example, not only did they want to be on film like the Beatles, but they also appeared many times on television. Moreover, probably inspired by the success of the Monkees television series, which debuted on September 12, 1966, and aired its final episode on March 25, 1968, the Who even toyed with the idea of their own television series both in late 1966 and early 1968.[7] Still, they came close to being on film during this period. Italian film director Michelangelo Antonioni wanted the band in his 1966 film *Blow-Up* but ended up with the Yardbirds, who in turn imitated the Who's "auto-destruction" of their instruments in the film.[8]

The Who's schizophrenic relationship with the music industry and the commercialization of popular music can be summarized by a statement made by their guitarist, Pete Townshend, in 1968: "Pop music is crucial to today's art, and it's crucial that it should remain art, and it's crucial that it should progress as art."[9] Thus, there is a tension in the Who between producing music that makes the industry increasing profits and producing music that marks its progress as an art. In these terms, selling out as a musician for the Who means producing music that seeks only to maximize the profits of the music industry—and, of course, hopefully, the band too.

This is further complicated in the case of the Who because their first record contract was a bad one. Their hunt for a record deal ended when their managers, Lambert and Stamp, gained the attention of the American record producer Shel Talmy in 1964, who was at the time admired for his early work with the Kinks. Talmy contracted the Who to a six-year deal that gave him the freedom to license his acts to record companies. Through his efforts, the Who had a deal with Decca records in the United States and its UK subsidiary Brunswick records. Problem was that although they now had a record deal, its royalty rate was a paltry 2.5 percent, and to make matters worse, it afforded Talmy a great deal of artistic control. A legal battle over this contract ensued in early 1966 and would have catastrophic financial consequences for them for years to come.

The Who's first album, *My Generation*, was released in the United Kingdom by Brunswick records on December 4, 1965, and released in the United States by Decca records in April 1966 as *The Who Sings My Generation*.[10] The Who's legal battle was with the band's first producer, Talmy and Brunswick Records, with whom they had recorded three singles in 1965 ("I Can't Explain," "Anyway Anyhow Anywhere," and "My Generation") and the *My Generation* album. The outcome was that the Who got out of their contract and gained artistic freedom and could at least record in the United Kingdom without compromise, but Talmy won 5 percent of all of the band's future recording work up until 1971. Lambert and Stamp then founded their own label, Track Records, a move that was ahead of even the Beatles' Apple label.[11]

As a result of the lawsuit, their second album, *A Quick One*, was released in the United Kingdom by Reaction Records on December 3, 1966, and as *Happy Jack* in the United States by Decca in May 1967. It would be Kit Lambert's first sustained production work on an album. The production of the record, compared to Talmy's efforts, is much more sober. Lambert leveled out the instruments and avoided the fiery bursts of chaos found in Talmy's production.[12] Reaction Records was a temporary label until Lambert and Stamp could launch Track Records, which though an independent label, was operated through a production deal with Polydor Records.[13]

The conditions then for *The Who Sell Out* were quite unique and speak directly to what was put to vinyl. *The Who Sell Out* came at the tail end of a bitter lawsuit with their first producer and record label and was released on a label newly founded by their managers, both of whom had little experience within the music industry. Moreover, it would also be produced by Lambert and Stamp, with the former listed as "Producer" and the latter as "Executive Producer." It is safe to say, that *The Who Sell Out* would never have found its way to vinyl if it were not for these major conditions: self-production and self-publishing.

One of the more unusual aspects of the album is its use of "pirate radio." Music critic John Atkins says that it is both

a homage to and a parody of the semilegal offshore radio stations that had defined the sound of the mid-1960s in Britain, such as Radio Caroline and particularly Radio London. Nothing was spared (good or bad) in the Who's satirical recreation of Radio London: vulgarity of the commercials, the inane jingles that punctuated the music, and the thrill of the exciting new sounds that emanated through the airwaves. This is a radio station that plays constant Who music, of course, though to give the right impression, the band sequenced a selection of songs that reflected a wide range of styles and arrangements.[14]

Ben Toney, the former program director of Radio London took umbrage to the term *pirate* in reference to radio stations like his. He notes that before Radio London hit the air in December of 1964, "the major record companies and the Performing Rights Society formed a pact and unofficially declared that they would not recognize the so-called 'pirates.' Their contention was that the pirates gave too much exposure to records and thus reduced their sales potential."[15] The growth of these pirate radio stations thus challenged the long-held control of the music industry by powerful companies like EMI and Decca. Writes Toney, "The BBC was meaningless for record promotion because the Performing Rights Society demanded that they play any one record only once daily. Before the 'pirates' came along, only Radio Luxembourg was available as a promotion outlet and since EMI and Decca purchased between them the greater number of hours on that station, they ruled the industry."[16] But pirate stations, like Radio London, whose one-year profits "had cleared close to $7,000,000" were challenging the status quo in the music industry.[17]

Radio London (also called "Wonderful Radio London" and "Big L") was an all-day Top 40 offshore commercial radio station that operated from a ship anchored in the North Sea, three and one-half miles off of Frinton-on-Sea, Essex, England. It operated from December 23, 1964, to August 14, 1967. Broadcast from the MV *Galaxy*, a former World War II United States Navy minesweeper, it was shut down at 3 p.m. on August 14, 1967, only hours before the Marine Broadcasting Offences Act of 1967 came into effect at midnight, which made it illegal to broadcast music without a license from ships like the MV *Galaxy*. At its peak, Radio London had twelve million listeners in the United Kingdom and another four million in the Netherlands, Belgium, and France.[18]

The context of pirate radio and the history of Radio London

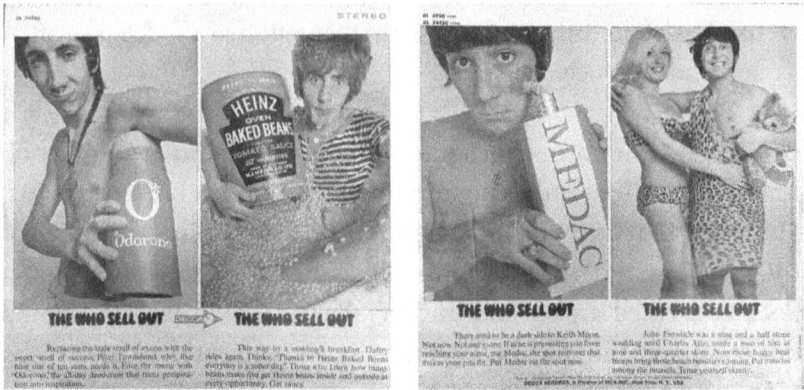

Front cover (left) and back cover (right) of the Who, *The Who Sell Out* (Decca Records, DL 74950 [stereo]. Released January 6, 1968).

specifically provides an important context for understanding the Who's critique on *The Who Sell Out*. Side one of the album mixes ads and jingles with songs and plays like a continuous radio program. The only thing not heard on the vinyl is a disc jockey (like the ones used by Radio London). Some of the ads and jingles are authentic ones that were played on Radio London,[19] and some of them were made up by the Who. So too are some of the products advertised real items, whereas others were fabricated by the band.[20]

The radio and product advertising satire though starts with the album cover that has photos of each of the four members of the band advertising a product with some accompanying ad copy. On the front cover, there is a photo of Pete Townshend rubbing a huge tube of "Odorono" deodorant under his arm with the ad copy, "Replacing the stale smell of excess with the sweet smell of success, Peter Townshend . . . needs it. Face the music with Odorono, the all-day deodorant that turns perspiration into inspiration." Also on the front cover is a photo of Roger Daltrey sitting in tub filled with baked beans and holding its oversized can with the caption "This way to a cowboy's breakfast. Daltry [sic] rides again. Thinks: 'Thanks to Heinz Baked Beans everyday is a super day.' Those who know how many beans make five get Heinz beans inside and outside at every opportunity. Get saucy." On the back cover are photos of Keith Moon hawking acne cream and John Entwistle pitching the Charles Atlas weightlifting program. Although each photo is related to a song (or "ad" song) on the album, there is no listing of any of the songs on the album jacket, which was a first for LP records. So too was the featuring of unflattering photos of band members on the album jacket, in this instance, dealing with some of their body "issues": odor, acne, muscle tone, and dribbling of beans.

Side one has six songs interspersed with radio ads. It begins with a radio announcement of the days of the week, "Monday" through "Saturday" (but no "Sunday"). "Armenia City in the Sky," the first cut, is sung by Roger Daltrey. It is a psychedelic song with an assortment of backwards instruments à la the Beatles' "Tomorrow Never Knows" (1966). It is followed by a fifty-seven-second ad for Heinz Baked Beans that includes an inane horn bit. It spoofs family life with lines like, "What's for Tea, Mum?" "Mary Anne with the Shaky Hand" is a pop song with a three-part vocal harmony in the model of the Everly Brothers. It is followed by a Keith Moon ad for Premier drums. "Odorono," sung by Pete Townshend, is a cautionary tale about personal hygiene named after something that was once a real product: "Deodorant let her down, she should have used Odorono," sings Townshend. It is followed by an ad for Radio London. "Tattoo," sung by Daltrey, "examines the pressures exerted by society on individuals to conform, one result of which is that men tattoo their bodies to enhance their manliness."[21] It is followed by an ad reminding you to go to church—even if "Sunday" is not one of the days of the week announced by the ad at the start of the album, "Radio London reminds you to go to the church of your choice."

The fifth song on side one, "Our Love Was, Is," sung by Townshend, covers a rare topic for the Who but is an appropriate one for 1967 and its "summer of love." But the use of the past tense is probably a jab by the Who at the euphoria of the summer of love.

It is followed by a number of ads including an ad for Rotosound strings by John Entwistle. "I Can See for Miles" was released as a single on October 14, 1967, two months before the album came out, although it was written in 1966. It was the most powerful, complex song they had written to date. It is the last cut on side one and is not followed up by an ad. Although the song is commonly said to have been written by Townshend about his future wife, Karen, inspired by the jealousy and fear of leaving her when he went away on tour, as the last song on side one, it can also in the context of the album be associated with seeing land from the MV *Galaxy*, which was anchored three and one-half miles off the coast of England.

Side two also has six songs but does not follow the same radio ad format as side one. Like side one, side two begins with an ad. This one is a mock country ad for the Charles Atlas course that can turn you "into a beast of a man." It is voiced by Pete Townshend "before" the man is turned into a beast and by John Entwistle "after" the man becomes a beast. "I Can't Reach You," the first song on side two, is an up-tempo pop song sung by Townsend. It is followed by a fifty-seven-second ad for an acne cream, Medac, voiced by John Entwistle. On the US release of the LP, the ad is called "Spotted Henry" rather than "Medac," as on the UK release. "Relax" is an anthem to hedonism, with a short guitar solo that when played live could go on for ten minutes. Noticeably, there is no ad after this song. "Silas Stingy" is a song about a man who spends so much money protecting his fortune that he finds he has spent it all. Its message seems to be "Don't worry about money, it's not important; but if you want to hoard it, use a bank." Again, there is no ad after this song. "Sunrise" is a complex and delicate song sung by Townshend and is played on an acoustic guitar. Again, there is no ad after this song. "Rael," the final cut on the album, is a political fable that addresses the issue of overpopulation and concerns the discovery of new lands and the idealism of an explorer. The explorer in this song is betrayed by his crew when they don't return to pick him up. After this song there are three short bits of identical repeated sound. It is hard to tell if they are from a song or an ad. While much there is much humor and satire about contemporary consumer culture and modern life in many of the songs and ads, they are all dwarfed by the aspirations of "Rael."

In the first few months of 1967, Townshend started to compose an opera. It would be about a man during a world takeover by the Chinese. There would be twenty-five scenes, and it would be set in 1999. "The hero," explains Townshend in the magazine *Beat Instrumental* in March of 1967, "goes through hundreds of different situations and there is music for each." "He goes out in a boat and gets shipwrecked, he has a bad nightmare and so on. I have used sound effects for a lot of the situations with music over them."[22] Within a few months, his aspirations where truncated to a shorter opera entitled *Rael.* "The opera," Townshend tells the same magazine in August of 1967, "would last a good 20–30 minutes so I don't know if we could use it on the next LP. It would take up too much of the record."[23]

The version of *Rael* on *The Who Sell Out* is the result of editing down twenty to thirty minutes of music to the length of a 45 rpm single. Says Townshend, "Basically the story was running into about twenty scenes when Kit Lambert reminded me that while I was pretending to be Wagner, The Who needed a new single. What did I have? I had 'Rael.' Thus 'Rael' was edited down to four minutes (too long for a single in those days ironically) and recorded in New York for that purpose. It later appeared on an album. No one will ever know what it means, it has been squeezed up too tightly to make sense."[24] Music critics are enamored with *The Who Sell Out* primarily because of the novelty of using radio ads and jingles. Many too are disappointed that the ads and jingles do not extend through the entire second side of the album. Thus, they regard it as an incomplete concept album if the concept was to mimic a radio station complete with commercials. But as a critique of consumer society, and the use of music and radio in the promotion of consumption, they do more than enough work on the album even if the Medac acne commercial is the last radio advertisement on the album. Note, however, this last ad is then followed by an anthem to hedonism ("Relax"), a song about the perils of hoarding money ("Silas Stingy"), and a delicate acoustic number ("Sunrise").

Arguably these three songs set the stage for escaping from the corporate sound machine and the rabid commercialization that is part of the music industry. It is fitting then that the album ends with a truncated utopian opera ("Rael"). Recall that the theme of the original "Rael" was escape from an overpopulated world; the album itself up to this point is also a kind of escape from the over-commercialized music industry, in which sound is just another product like baked beans, acne medication, and tattoos. The ads on drum sticks and bass strings take the focus from the music to advertising the literal instruments of music production. According to the Who, everything is sold out in our world: bodies, music, love, and pleasure. It might be argued then that the four closing songs ("Relax," "Silas Stingy," "Sunrise," and "Rael") aspire to set the tone for exploring a world beyond the corporate one. That it is only expressed in fragments is the frustration of moving beyond the music industry and capitalism.

The Who, however, were not just satirizing others for selling out on *The Who Sell Out*. Nor were they simply biting the musical (industry) hand that was feeding them. They were pointing to a form of sell out that transcends its standard connotations of financial expediency. The Who recognized that, like it or not, they were part of a music industry that commercializes every aspect of itself. Although their experiences with their first record deal allowed them to recoup some of their artistic freedom, it did not mean that they were completely free from the control of the music industry. More precisely, their artistic freedom even as independent record producers did not extend to making the entire second side of *The Who Sell Out* consist merely of the long version of "Rael." Even with their own self-produced music, concessions needed to be made.

However, in fading out the ads and jingles, and including albeit in truncated form a piece that rejected the pop music format in its initial operatic form, the Who were suggesting an alternative or solution to the pop industry of the 1950s and 1960s. It would be the "rock opera," a new form of rock and roll music, that would in turn generate an entirely new set of complaints about music in the 1970s.

Unlike say the folk singers of the 1960s, such as Joan Baez and Pete Seeger, or like some other rock artists, like Frank Zappa and the Mothers of Invention, who all regarded themselves as somehow outside of the music industry and society that they were critiquing, the Who on *The Who Sell Out* did not.[25] This created a problem for them: whereas Seeger, Baez, and Zappa would forge careers out of critiquing the corporatization of youth through the music and culture industries, the Who found it difficult to produce studio work that would surpass *The Who Sell Out* in terms of its critical power.

Their next studio album, *Tommy*, released on May 23, 1969, was a rock opera that became their first million-selling album. But like much of their work, opinion was polarized on it. One critic called it a "disappointment . . . pretension is too strong a word; maybe over-ambitious is the right term, but sick certainly does apply."[26] Barry Miles said "[i]t is impossible to praise this album too highly . . . The Who . . . have pulled together the threads of Rock & Roll, progressive pop, social comment and present philosophical developments till they have crystallised into this one project—a massive undertaking. . . . The Who are ahead of everyone!"[27] Nevertheless, *Tommy* was not a meta-musical critique of the music industry. Rather it would foreshadow the excesses of rock music in the 1970s in its pretension and grandiosity. Still *The Who Sell Out*'s "Rael" prepared us well for the Who music to come in both a philosophical and literal sense, as the instrumental theme in "Rael" was incorporated into *Tommy* in two of its songs, "Sparks" and "Underture."

WE'RE ONLY IN IT FOR THE MONEY

It should be clear from my discussion of *The Who Sell Out* that this particular album provides a strange albeit powerful vision of selling out. On the one hand, it mocks a music industry that monetizes everything; whereas on the other, it suggests by its very musical being that moving beyond the industry norms is possible (though difficult). But to see in *The Who Sell Out* a parallel with say the way Derrida sells out Western metaphysics in his 1967 theoretical trilogy is to posit a very high musical and theoretical bar for selling out. It is also to put a target on your back as both the work of the Who on this album and Derrida in his early deconstruction may be viewed as pointing a judgmental finger respectively toward both the music and philosophy industries.

Some might argue that selling out music is nothing like selling out theory. They might maintain that one needs to perform a sleight of hand to move from selling out in the music industry to selling in out in the theory industry. But for others, the basic moves appear similar—and the cross-comparison yields more clarity regarding both industries. Albums are comparable to books, singles are like articles, and a live performance is akin to the classroom. So why not place them in dialogue? Especially when it comes to efforts to understand how, when, and why we sell out as theorists in particular, if not as academics in general.

Derrida set the stage for the selling out of philosophy and the humanities to theory like no other person of his era with the publication of three seminal books in 1967: *Of Grammatology*, *Speech and Phenomena*, and *Writing and Difference*. These works outline the possibilities of a deconstruction of a metaphysics of presence and describe the effects of logocentrism and phonocentrism in the Western canon. They gave deconstruction a scholarly backbone and launched a thousand ships of commentators, both favorable and unfavorable.[28] With the publication of these works, Derrida came to be one of the major lightning rods of theory, accused of destroying everything from philosophy to the humanities in general. His critiques of philosophical standards such as Plato's *Phaedrus* and Rousseau's *Confessions* is comparable to the Who's critiques of psychedelic music and pirate radio on *The Who Sell Out*.

But just as the Who did not act alone in their critique of the music industry, neither did Derrida regarding the philosophy industry. That is to say, just as there were other artists at the time offering similar critiques of the music industry through their recordings, most prominent among them Frank Zappa and the Mothers of Invention,[29] so too were other intellectuals in 1967 offering similar critiques of the philosophy industry through their publications. Richard Rorty edited an anthology entitled *The Linguistic Turn* in 1967, which brought together a range of analytic philosophers who were challenging some of the metaphysical traditions in philosophy, in the same year that Roland Barthes published his influential essay "The Death of the Author" and the novelist John Barth published "The Literature of Exhaustion." Therefore, not only was Western philosophy being sold out in 1967, so too was the author and the novel. And, arguably, just a year later, this all would come to a head with the student and worker uprisings of 1968, which sought to define new identities in relation to the institutions and industries of the family, the state, and education.

Still, it must be acknowledged that all efforts to define new identities in relation to industries and institutions are not the same. This holds just as well for the family, the state, and education as it does for music and theory. The term *sell out* creates a sort of fault line or divide between pursuing these new identities with integrity (the high bar) and pursuing them without integrity (the low bar). But, as we see in the case of the Who's album and Derrida's early deconstruction, forging new identities with integrity does not entail simply rejecting one's musical and philosophical roots. Rather, it involves both embracing these roots and moving beyond them, which is something that at least one definition of sell out confirms.

The top definition of 169 proposed definitions of a *sell out* according to the Urban Dictionary is "anyone who sacrifices artistic integrity in an effort to become more successful or popular (generally in music); someone who forgets their roots."[30] In other words, not being a musical sell out involves both being true to your artistic integrity and acknowledging your roots—exactly what the Who did on their album *The Who Sell Out.* Thus, there is an irony at the root of the use of *sell out* in reference to the Who that one does not find in its more popular usage in which the musician either is not true to their artistic integrity or forgets their roots or both. In music, some popular examples of musicians that have allegedly sold out in this way are the punk band Green Day (because they were on MTV), Metallica (because they "bitched about their fans trading their music online"), and even Bob Dylan (because he is in an iPod ad).[31]

It is interesting of course to see how popular conceptions of selling out in music function. A punk band who does videos for cable television is dubbed a sell out; so too is a metal band that did not take too favorably to free download access to their music. And then there is Dylan, who probably has more frequently than any other popular musical artist been accused of selling out and who has an origin story in this regard dating back to the evening of Sunday, July 25, 1965, when he sold out folk music by opening his set at the Newport Folk Festival with an electric version of "Maggie's Farm."[32]

Just on the basis then of the three musical examples above (Green Day, Metallica, and Dylan) and the definition of *sell out* noted above, we can start to put a picture together of how one can sell out theory. Like Green Day, if one starts giving popular lectures such as TED Talks aimed at the general public as a theorist, one risks being called a sell out; like Metallica, if one "bitches about their students getting their books online for free," they risk being called a sell out; and like Dylan, if they give up one form of theory suddenly for another allegedly just to garner attention, then they risk being called a sell out. But there are of course many more ways to commodify theory and to transfer it into more popular registers.

For one, every time we give a live performance of theory in our classroom, we risk sacrificing our intellectual integrity by transferring it into a register that will reach our students. This situation is amplified by the fact that our "sacrifice" is done with the aim of pleasing our students lest they complain about our teaching performance or the unreasonable difficulty of theory. Moreover, in the neoliberal university, where the humanities are judged by their ability to train students for a vocation, if our live performances of theory in the classroom do not cover its professional applications, then we risk losing the stage of our theory classrooms. Thus, in the live performance of theory in the classroom we are confronted with a dual-headed imperative to sell it out through application: first as a means of assuring the effective teaching of theory to students who are not motivated to learn it and second as a means of demonstrating its relevance to the vocational telos of the neoliberal academy.[33]

Furthermore, the drive to sell out theory to more popular registers is not just limited to the classroom but also extends to the world of publishing. This is particularly true of many of the major presses that support the publication of theory: Oxford University Press, Routledge, Johns Hopkins University Press, Bloomsbury, University of Minnesota Press, and Norton, for example, all publish a variety of textbooks, handbooks, companions, anthologies, and guidebooks in support of the theory industry. Their aim is to increase the audience for theory by presenting it in a format that softens its intellectual rigor. Although this is not unique to theory, as one finds in, for example, philosophy as well, it is perhaps next to our classroom performances the most dominant register for selling out theory.

The story here is amplified though when the person who is publishing in these popular registers is both a distinguished theorist and appears to be popularizing theory primarily or solely as a means to personal, professional, or financial gain. While I'm fairly confident that theorists such as Jacques Lacan, Julia Kristeva, Hélène Cixous, Jean-François Lyotard, Gilles Deleuze, Michel Foucault, and Jacques Derrida could never be accused of this type of selling out of theory, there are a number of major theorists for which a case could be made here.

One such theorist is said to have grown up poor and has been valiantly dubbed in the press as a "class warrior." As a youth, this theorist was an encyclopedia salesman who studied at Trinity College, where one of his classmates was Prince Charles, who described him as "dreadful." Later, he came to be "widely regarded as Britain's leading literary theorist"[34] and "the man who succeeded F. R. Leavis as Britain's most influential academic critic"[35] and was on the faculty of Oxford University for three decades, where he eventually held the Thomas Warton professorship in English literature from 1992 to 2001. In 2001, he surprised the academic world by leaving Oxford to take up the John Edward Taylor Professorship in English Literature at the University of Manchester, where he remained until 2008, when he became a Distinguished Professor of English Literature at Lancaster University, where he remains. His name is Terry Eagleton.

Among literary theorists, there is nary one among us that does not have strong feelings about Eagleton and his work, especially the textbook he published in 1983 that brought him international attention. Eagleton largely established his reputation through the publication of *Literary Theory: An Introduction*, which became a surprise best seller, with sales figures of over 750,000 copies sold in just its first two decades of publication history. Today its sales figures exceed one million copies sold, and it has been translated into Malay, Arabic, and Sanskrit, among other languages.

Since *Literary Theory*'s publication, Eagleton has become the poster professor for popularizing literary theory. In his 2001 memoir, *The Gatekeeper*, Eagleton says that his work as an encyclopedia salesman was his "earliest experience of peddling ideas to the masses, a project which later became my full-time occupation."[36] In an interview the same year, he said, "I believe in popularizing and believe I can do it quite well," but he is nevertheless aware, writes Helen Davies, "that such successful popularising of the theories of others can gain a book a reputation, as a 'bluffer's guide' to what is still a trendy, tricky, and comparatively new academic subject."[37]

In spite of the success of *Literary Theory* in the classroom, Eagleton has always maintained that he did not set out to write a "textbook." His "real motive for writing the book," he tells Davies, "was a 'democratic impulse,' which stemmed from his undergraduate days at Cambridge in the early 1960s." "I studied in the final days when to appreciate literature was rather like knowing fine wines, it came with breeding," says Eagleton to Davies. He viewed this as "an elitist approach which tended to exclude a boy from Salford with Irish roots like himself," says Davies. His third-generation Irish immigrant family was so poor in Eagleton's youth that "his two brothers died in infancy," and all he and his "classmates had to eat at lunchtime was beetroot, which they would puke up in the afternoons."[38] In short, Eagleton characterizes his efforts to popularize literary theory as a form of class warfare, wherein his work makes it accessible to those without "breeding."

"I have tried to popularize, rather than vulgarize, the subject," writes Eagleton in the preface to *Literary Theory*.[39] "There are some who complain that literary theory is impossibly esoteric—who suspect it as an arcane, elitist enclave somewhat akin to nuclear physics," he continues. "It is true that a 'literary education' does not exactly encourage analytical thought; but literary theory is in fact no more difficult than many theoretical enquiries, and a good deal easier than some. I hope the book may help to demystify those who fear that the subject is beyond their reach."[40] If we believe Eagleton, *Literary Theory* was an effort to "democratize" theory and make it more accessible to students and a general audience. But in spite of Eagleton's position at Oxford and his renown as a literary theorist, there are many who view him as selling-out theory in order to achieve academic renown and financial gain. Moreover, the fact that he is a Marxist seems to only amplify things. Here is a representative sample of this type of complaint: "Eagleton wishes for capitalism's demise, but as long as it's here, he plans to do as well as he can out of it. Someone who owns three homes shouldn't be preaching self-sacrifice, and someone whose career-ism at Oxbridge was legendary shouldn't be telling interviewers of his longstanding regret at having turned down a job at the Open University."[41] So, the cost of making a career out of successfully translating theory into a mainstream register is to reap the scorn of those who say that as a Marxist, Eagleton should not benefit from capitalism at the same time as working toward its demise. While Eagleton views such criticisms as shallow cheap shots and summarily dismisses them, such criticism of a man who called himself "the worm in Thatcher's apple" becomes in turn "the worm in Eagleton's theoretical apple."

But this is not the only worm. For some, Eagleton sold out theory again in his 2003 book, *After Theory*, in which he argued that the ambitiousness and originality of high theory has given way to the laziness and derivativeness of the current orthodoxies of cultural theory. Whereas high theory was formed out of a real sensitivity to the social and political realities of the 1960s, current cultural theory appears to Eagleton to be born out of attempts to be merely fashionably obscure. For example, in *After Theory*, Eagleton bemoans that although high theory established the body as a locus of cultural theory, it was the laboring and famished body, not the erotic and coupling body. Whereas sexuality and gender began as two of the "towering achievements" of cultural theory, over the years they have been reduced to seemingly intellectual amusements. Moreover, in *After Theory*, he comes close to presenting himself as an anti-theorist in his defense of absolute truth, objectivity, virtue, and morality in cultural theory. For many current theorists, Eagleton's book was not only an assault on their orthodoxies; it was also an assault on the orthodoxies that he himself was largely responsible for introducing to a wider public back in the early 1980s. In short, whether it was popularizing theory in the early 1980s or trying to unpopularize it in the early 2000s, the Marxist with three homes epitomized the lowest form of selling out theory from the highest levels of academe—that is, until Rita Felski came along a few years ago to challenge Eagleton for the honor.

Despite the best efforts of the poster professor for the popularization of theory trying to undo his own work and become the poster professor for unpopularizing theory in his 2003 book *After Theory*, Eagleton met his match with Felski when she became the poster professor for attempting to unpopularize theory. Her high profile and higher funded antitheory movement, initiated just a few years ago, is an effort to move beyond the critique that Eagleton and others successfully made accessible to several generations of students as well as to a general audience back in the 1980s and 1990s.

Felski's post-critique came in the form of a $4.2 million grant in 2016 from the Danish National Research Foundation. A press release from her university announcing the grant says that it stems from work done in her 2015 book, *The Limits of Critique*, which "encouraged her fellow scholars to explore alternatives to increasingly predictable and formulaic styles of 'suspicious reading.'"[42] Felski, continues the release, says "literary scholars should spend less time looking behind a text for hidden causes and suspicious motives and more time placing themselves in front of it to reflect on what it suggests, unfolds or makes possible. What literary studies needs, she said, is less emphasis on 'de' words—demystifying, debunking, deconstructing—and more emphasis on 're' words—literature's potential to remake, reshape and recharge perception."[43] Felski claims that she will use the grant to "develop new frameworks and methods for exploring the many social uses of literature," something she has already begun in her course, "Theories of Reading," where, "students first learn to become skeptical readers, drawing on ideas from Freud, Foucault or feminism to criticize the works of the canon or to challenge their assumptions of their favorite TV shows" and then learn "to reflect on why they love certain novels or movies and to develop more sophisticated vocabularies for describing and justifying these feelings."[44]

Felski's comments here are important to note because they betray the basic parameters of her antitheory. For her, theory has become "predicable and formulaic," and she aims to provide it with "new frameworks and methods." These new "frameworks and methods," that is to say, "antitheories," will establish "more sophisticated vocabularies for describing and justifying" why we "love certain novels and movies"—and, of course, television shows.

Arguably, Felski builds her post-critique on the foundation of the success of efforts like Eagleton's to demystify and popularize theory. But her effort to place "more emphasis on 're' words—literature's potential to remake, reshape and recharge perception" comes with a bit of irony, especially when we consider that Eagleton opens up *Literary Theory* with the statement, "If one wanted to put a date on the beginnings of the transformation which has overtaken literary theory this century, one could do worse than settle on 1917, the year the young Russian Formalist Viktor Shklovsky published his pioneering essay, 'Art as Device'"[45]—a piece which introduces the concepts of defamiliarization, foregrounding, and estrangement, arguing that art is a means to make things real again, that is to say, a means of recharging our perception of things. Hence, from Shklovsky in 1917 to Felski in 2017, literary theory has come full circle back to its fabled beginnings through a series of high- and low-profile sell outs.

CONCLUSION

All sell outs are not the same. Those who sell out theory through critique are doing the highest work of theory. Such sell outs are generational affairs and not everyday ones. Albums like *The Who Sell Out* or Derrida's 1967 "deconstruction" trilogy, though sell outs of the highest order, aim to push the respective music and theory industries to new directions. Although not sell outs in the popular sense of the term because their ostensive aim is not solely personal, professional, or financial gain, and they have not "forgotten" their roots, they still function as sell outs. Perhaps the best way to think of them is as critical sell outs in that they do not sacrifice artistic integrity or forget their roots but rather become popular because of their integrity and the way they critically uproot the work of their peers and predecessors. Because uprooting the music and theory industries effects its membership, these reverse sell outs draw a lot of attention and controversy.

As opposed to critical sell outs, the more popular and established form of selling out, that is, using music or theory solely as a means to personal, professional, or financial gain by sacrificing one's critical integrity in an effort to become popular or successful, and forgetting one's roots, might be called an uncritical or neoliberal sell out. If one's only value consideration is their place in the marketplace of music or theory, then the market determines both one's integrity and artistic and/or intellectual telos.

Uncritical selling out though becomes academic business as usual for the docile subjects of neoliberal academe.[46] Rather than using theory to critically undermine the neoliberal education industry, uncritical theory sell outs only serve to bolster it. And, given the recent downturn in tenure-track positions available for literary theorists, they appear to be succeeding. It has recently been reported that from 1995 to 1999, there were thirty tenure-track jobs available for literary theorists, compared to only five available from 2015 to 2018.[47]

Uncritical sell outs like Eagleton's and Felski's though have more impact with respect to this decline than everyday live classroom theory sell outs. Why? Because the public transition from theorist to antitheorist by some of theory's former champions serve to legitimate claims of the wastefulness of theory. These acts of uncritical selling out are the lowest forms of selling out.

English and literary studies have squandered through uncritical sell outs the opportunity provided to them to make their departments the locus of critical theory in the university. The odd result is that while their departments have fewer opportunities for tenure-track positions in the area of theory, most other areas of the university seem to be busting out with interest in theory. My conclusion here is that while literary theory may have reached its nadir in the academy, theory has moved in the opposite direction. All of those "studies" that Eagleton despises have spread like a fever across the disciplines. And the more that Felski uses her millions of dollars in grant money to forward post-critique, the stronger critique seems to be in every area of the university except in English and literature departments.

The more fully we acquiesce to requests to be more accessible, more relevant, more pragmatic, more concrete, and, finally, more democratic in our theoretical modes of analysis, the more deeply we will descend into the realm of uncritically selling out theory. Although each of these uncritical sell outs may only seem like drops of water taken out of the ocean of theory, critical climate change has brought to us a greater appreciation of the potentially massive scale of small acts. When we uncritically sell out theory in our classroom, we sell out the future of democratic education and further extend the lifespan of the neoliberal university. Who then sells out theory? At its highest level and lowest levels, the names are recognizable, but at its everyday level, it is everyone who walks into a classroom willing to sacrifice their theoretical integrity in an effort to become more successful or popular with their students—and who forgets the critical roots of theory in the process.

Notes

PREFACE

1. The first compact disc was pressed on August 17, 1982. Some consider this the day that the compact disc officially began to take the place of vinyl.

2. According to the documentary *I Need That Record! The Death (or Possible Survival) of the Independent Record Store* (2008; dir. Brendan Toller), from 1998 to 2008, over three thousand independent record stores closed in the United States. By comparison, the number of independent bookstores was also greatly reduced over the past twenty-five years—about 2,321 remain as of 2019 as compared to nearly seven thousand in the mid-nineties. In 2014, there were about two thousand, so the number has risen a bit over the past five years. See Jeffrey R. Di Leo, *The End of American Literature: Essays from the Late Age of Print* (Huntsville, TX: Texas Review Press, 2019), 159–64.

3. See here the excellent documentary *All Things Must Pass: The Rise and Fall of Tower Records* (2015; dir. Colin Hanks).

4. "2017 U.S. Music Year-End Report," *Nielsen,* January 3, 2018. https://www.nielsen.com/us/en/insights/report/2018/2017-music-us-year-end-report/.

5. Chris Morris, "As Vinyl Surges, a Boutique Pressing Plant Helps Smaller Indies Get an In," *Variety,* April 23, 2018. https://variety.com/2018/music/news/vinyl-record-pressing-plant-fills-lp-niche-1202784124/.

6. Vish Khanna, "Why Aren't There More Vinyl Pressing Plants?" *Pitchfork,* June 9, 2014. https://pitchfork.com/thepitch/363-why-arent-there-more-vinyl-pressing-plants/amp/.

7. As of 2019, there are twenty-nine record manufacturing plants in the United States. See https://www.gottagrooverecords.com, which runs one of these plants, for a list of every vinyl record press in the United States. In 2014, by

comparison, when Khanna asked the question above, there were only about twenty.

8. Friedrich A. Kittler, *Gramophone, Film, Typewriter*, trans. Geoffrey Winthrop-Young and Michael Wutz (Stanford, CA: Stanford University Press, 1999). See my review of this book in *The Comparatist* 25 (2001): 176–78.

9. See, for example, the documentaries, *Vinyl* (2000, dir. Alan Zweig); *Scratch* (2001; dir. Doug Pray); *Desperate Man Blues: Discovering the Roots of American Music* (2003; dir. Edward Gillan); *John Peel's Record Box* (2005; dir. Elaine Shepherd); *I Need That Record! The Death (or Possible Survival) of the Independent Record Store* (2008; dir. Brendan Toller); *Red Beans and Rice* (2010; prod. Christine Kirkley); *Record Store Day: The Documentary* (2011; dir. Jason Wilder Evans); *Re-Vinylized* (2011; dir. John Boston); *Sound It Out* (2011, dir. Jeanie Finlay); *Vinylmania: When Life Runs at 33 Revolutions per Minute* (2012; dir. Paolo Campana); *Last Shop Standing: The Rise, Fall and Rebirth of the Independent Record Shop* (2012; dir. Pip Piper); *When Albums Ruled the World* (2013; dir. Steve O'Hagan); *Our Vinyl Weighs a Ton: This Is Stones Throw Records* (2013; dir. Jeff Broadway); *Records Collecting Dust* (2015, dir. Jason Blackmore); and *All Things Must Pass: The Rise and Fall of Tower Records* (2015; dir. Colin Hanks).

10. 78 rpm records, which usually measure 10 inches in diameter, were produced between about 1898 and the late 1950s. They spin at a rate of 78 revolutions per minute, which allows for a much shorter playing time than 33 1/3 rpm records, which usually measure 12 inches in diameter and started to become popular in the early 1950s. 33 1/3 rpm records allow for about 26 minutes per side, whereas 78 rpm records allow for about 5 minutes per side.

CHAPTER 1

1. Michel Foucault, *The History of Sexuality: Volume I: An Introduction*, trans. Robert Hurley (New York: Pantheon, 1978), 138; translation of *La volonté de savoir* (Paris: Editions Gallimard, 1976).

2. Otto Erich Deutsch, Mozart: *A Documentary Biography* (Stanford, CA: Stanford University Press, 1965), 455.

3. Miles Davis with Quincy Troupe, *Miles: The Autobiography* (New York: Simon and Schuster, 1989), 14.

4. Ibid., 28.

5. Ibid., 29.

6. Ibid., 30.

7. Ibid., 333.

8. Ibid., 333.
9. Ibid., 410.
10. Brian Massumi, *Politics of Affect* (Malden, MA: Polity, 2015), 211.
11. Ibid., 211.
12. Ibid., xi.
13. Gilles Deleuze and Félix Guattari, *A Thousand Plateaus: Capitalism and Schizo-phrenia*, trans. Brian Massumi (Minneapolis: University of Minnesota Press, 1987), 299; translation of *Capitalisme et Schizophrénie*, vol. 2 (Paris: Les Editions de Minuit, 1980).
14. Ibid., 299.
15. Ibid., 299.
16. Ibid., 299.
17. Ian Buchanan, "Introduction: Deleuze and Music." In *Deleuze and Music*, eds. Ian Buchanan and Marcel Swiboda (Edinburgh: Edinburgh University Press, 2004), 16.
18. Ibid., 16.
19. Friedrich Nietzsche, *Nietzsche contra Wagner*, in *The Portable Nietzsche*, ed. and trans. Walter Kaufmann (New York: Viking, 1954), 662.
20. Ibid., 662.
21. Ibid., 664.
22. *Twilight of the Idols* was published in January of 1889, shortly after his break-down. The Nietzsche epigraph of this book comes from *Twilight of the Idols*. He wrote this book, as well as four others (*The Case of Wagner, The Antichrist, Ecce Homo*, and *Nietzsche contra Wagner*), in 1888, the most productive year of his life.
23. Friedrich Nietzsche, *The Case of Wagner*, in *The Birth of Tragedy and The Case of Wagner*, trans. Walter Kaufman (New York: Vintage, 1967), 164. This last sentence ends in a long dash, not a period.
24. Nietzsche, *Case of Wagner*, 165.
25. Friedrich Nietzsche, *Ecce Homo*, in *On the Genealogy of Morals and Ecce Homo*, trans. Walter Kaufman (New York: Vintage, 1969), 224.
26. Ibid., 224.
27. Nietzsche, *Case of Wagner*, 165n2.
28. Foucault did not lecture at the Collège de France during the 1976/1977 aca-demic year. The 1977/1978 lectures can be found in *Security, Territory, Pop-ulation: Lectures at the Collège de France, 1977–1978*, ed. Michael Senellart, trans. Braham Burchell (New York: Picador/Palgrave Macmillan, 2007), and 1978/1979 lectures in *The Birth of Biopolitics: Lectures at the Collège de France, 1978–1979*, ed. Michael Senellart, trans. Braham Burchell (New York: Picador/Palgrave Macmillan, 2008).

29. Michel Foucault, *"Society Must Be Defended": Lectures at the Collège de France, 1975–1976*, eds. Mauro Bertani and Alessandro Fontana, trans. David Macey (New York: Picador/Palgrave Macmillan, 2003), 243.
30. Ibid., 242.
31. Ibid., 242.
32. Ibid., 242–43.
33. Ibid., 243.
34. Ibid., 243.
35. Ibid., 243.
36. Ibid., 244.
37. Ibid., 244.
38. Ibid., 245.
39. Ibid., 245.
40. Ibid., 246.
41. Foucault, *History of Sexuality*, 138.
42. Ibid., 138.
43. Ibid., 138.
44. Ibid., 145.
45. Ibid., 142.
46. Nietzsche, *Nietzsche contra Wagner*, 664.
47. A classic example here is "Musak," which was "[c]reated in 1922 to provide music over the telephone, it branched out in 1940 into selling atmosphere music" (Jacques Attali, *Noise: The Political Economy of Music*, trans. Brian Massumi [Minneapolis: University of Minnesota Press, 1985], 111). Attali cites comments from David O'Neill, one of Musak's executive on the controlling influence of it in the workplace: "The current should go against the flow of professional fatigue. When the employee arrives in the morning, he is generally in a good mood, and the music will be calm. Toward ten thirty, he begins to feel a little tired, tense, so we give him a lift with the appropriate music. Toward the middle of the afternoon, he is probably feeling tired again: we wake him up again with a rhythmic tune, often faster than the morning's" (112).
48. Nietzsche, *Nietzsche contra Wagner*, 664. Pastilles Géraudel are a type of cough drops or throat lozenges popular at the time.
49. Massumi, *Politics of Affect*, 3–4.
50. Nietzsche, *Nietzsche contra Wagner*, 664.
51. Friedrich Nietzsche, *The Gay Science*, trans. Walter Kaufmann (New York: Vintage, 1974), 326.
52. Attali, *Noise*, 91.

53. This book was first published in 1977 by Presses Universitaires de France and later translated into English and published by the University of Minnesota Press in its pioneering and highly influential Theory and History of Literature series, edited by Wlad Godzich and Jochen Schulte-Sasse.

54. Attali, *Noise*, 25.

55. All biographical and bibliographical information on Attali comes from his personal website, http://www.attali.com.

56. Fredric Jameson, foreword to *Noise: The Political Economy of Music*, by Jacques Attali, trans. Brian Massumi (Minneapolis: University of Minnesota Press, 1985), xii.

57. http://www.attali.com..

58. Jameson, foreword, xii.

59. Ibid., xii.

60. Ibid., xii.

61. Ibid., xii.

62. Ibid., xiv.

63. Attali, *Noise*, 5.

64. Ibid., 87.

65. Ibid., 88; my emphasis.

66. Ibid., 89.

67. Ibid., 89.

68. Ibid., 88.

69. Ibid., 90.

70. Ibid., 88.

71. Ibid., 91; quoting Cros.

72. Ibid., 91.

73. Ibid., 92.

74. Ibid., 92.

75. Ibid., 92.

76. Ibid., 93; citing Edison.

77. Ibid., 94.

78. Ibid., 95.

79. Ibid., 94.

80. Ibid., 100.

81. Ibid., 100. It should be noted that that the "player piano," patented in 1897, is also a form of "repetition" albeit one not discussed by Attali. See "Player piano," https://www.britannica.com/art/player-piano.

82. Attali, *Noise*, 111.

83. Ibid., 100.

84. Ibid., 101.
85. Ibid., 101.
86. Ibid., 101.
87. Ibid., 101.
88. Ibid., 124.
89. Ibid., 126.
90. Ibid., 125.
91. Ibid., 127.
92. Ibid., 122.
93. Ibid., 122.
94. Ibid., 122.
95. Ibid., 122.
96. Ibid., 122.
97. Ibid., 122.
98. Ibid., 122.
99. Foucault, *Birth of Biopolitics*, 267–68.
100. Ibid., 268.
101. Ibid., 268.
102. Ibid., 226.
103. Ibid., 226.

CHAPTER TWO

1. Igor Stravinsky, *An Autobiography* (1936; New York: Norton, 1962), 150.
2. Michael Chanan, *Repeated Takes: A Short History of Recording and Its Effects on Music* (London: Verso, 1995), 117.
3. Stravinsky, *Autobiography*, 152. For Stravinsky, the ease of listening to the gramophone is even more apparent when compared to what Bach had to do to hear his own work: "In John Sebastian Bach's day it was necessary for him to walk ten miles to a neighboring town to hear Buxtenhude play his works" (152).
4. Theodor W. Adorno, "On Popular Music [With the assistance of George Simpson]," in *Essays on Music: Selected, with Introduction, Commentary, and Notes*, by Theodor W. Adorno, ed. Richard Leppert (Berkeley: University of California Press, 2002), 442.
5. Max Paddison, "The Critique Criticised: Adorno and Popular Music," *Popular Music* 2 (1982): 204.
6. Theodor W. Adorno, *Minima Moralia: Reflections from Damaged Life*, trans. E. F. N. Jephcott (1951; London: Verso, 1994), 147.

7. The poles of musical modernism were developed by Adorno most famously in his *Philosophy of Modern Music*, trans. Anne G. Mitchell and Wesley V. Blomster (1949; New York: The Seabury Press, 1973), with Stravinsky on one end of the spectrum and Schoenberg on the other.

8. Richard Leppert, introduction to *Essays on Music: Selected, with Introduction, Commentary, and Notes*, by Theodor W. Adorno, ed. Richard Leppert (Berkeley: University of California Press, 2002), 4.

9. Arnold Schoenberg lived and taught in Vienna between 1903 and 1925. The "circle" refers to the group of composers, conductors, and musicians who studied with him during this period. This "Second Vienna School" included Alban Berg, Anton Webern, Ernst Krenek, Heinrich Jalowetz, Erwin Stein, Egon Wellesz, Eduard Steuermann, Hanns Eisler, Roberto Gerhard, Norbert von Hannenheim, Rudolf Kolisch, Paul A. Pisk, Karl Rankl, Josef Rufer, Nikos Skalkottas, Viktor Ullmann, and Winfried Zillig. See René Leibowitz, *Schoenberg and His School: The Contemporary Stage of the Language of Music*, trans. Dika Newlin (New York: Philosophical Library, 1949). "Like Bach," writes Leibowitz, "Schoenberg succeeded in a great renewal; for just as the death of the modal system brought life to the tonal system, which was definitely constituted in the work of Bach, even so the classic tonal system, dead since Wagner, is transmuted, in Schoenberg's work, into [a] system" studied and practiced by the students in his "school" (286).

10. Alban Berg and Arnold Schoenberg, *The Berg-Schoenberg Correspondence: Selected Letters*, ed. Juliane Brand, Christopher Hailey, and Donald Harris, trans. Juliane Brand and Christopher Hailey (New York: Norton, 1987), 355; cited by Leppert, introduction, 14.

11. Adorno's opera was entitled *Der Schatz des Indianer-Joe* (*The Treasure of Indian-Joe*). Peter E. Gordon and Alexander Rehding, "Editors' Introduction: Adorno, Music, Modernity," *New German Critique* 43, no. 3 (2016): 2.

12. See, Max Horkheimer and Theodor W. Adorno, "The Culture Industry: Enlightenment as Mass Deception," in *Dialectic of Enlightenment: Philosophical Fragments*, trans. John Cumming (New York: Seabury Press, 1972), 120–67; originally published as *Philosophische fragmente* (New York: Social Studies Association, Inc., 1944).

13. Horkheimer and Adorno, "Culture Industry," 137.

14. My claim there is only further amplified by the recent reconstruction of his extensive work from 1939 to 1941 on radio, published in *Current of Music: Elements of a Radio Theory*. In short, radio as a means of musical reproduction was worthy of extensive investigation, whereas the phonograph was given only passing (largely dismissive) comment and a few brief early essays.

15. Richard Leppert, "Commentary," in *Essays on Music*, 232.

16. Horkheimer and Adorno, "Culture Industry," 137.

17. Leppert, "Commentary," 232.

18. Thomas Y. Levin, "For the Record: Adorno on Music in the Age of Its Technological Reproducibility," *October* 55 (Winter 1990): 27n13.

19. Theodor W. Adorno, "Zum *Anbruch*: Exposé," in *Gesammelte Schriften*, ed. Rolf Tiedemann et al., vol. 19, *Musikalische Schriften VI,* ed. Rolf Tiedemann (Frankfurt am Main: Suhrkamp, 1984), 601–2. Cited and translated by Levin, "For the Record," 27–28.

20. Levin, "For the Record," 28.

21. Theodor W. Adorno, "Zum Jahrgang 1929 des *Anbruch*," in *Gesammelte Schriften*, 19:607. Cited and translated by Levin, "For the Record," 29.

22. Theodor W. Adorno, "Nadelkurven," *Musikblätter des Anbruch* 10 (February 1928): 47–50.

23. Theodor W. Adorno, "Nadelkurven," *Phono: Internationale Schallplatten-Zeitschrift* 6 (July–August 1965): 123. Cited in Theodor W. Adorno, "The Curves of the Needle," trans. Thomas Y. Levin, *October* 55 (Winter 1990): 49.

24. Adorno, "Curves of the Needle," 49.

25. Ibid., 49.

26. Ibid., 49.

27. This work first appeared in *Zeitschrift für Sozialforschung* 5, no. 1 (1936). Reprinted in Walter Benjamin, *Illuminations*, ed. and intro. Hannah Arendt, trans. Harry Zohn (New York: Schocken Books, 1968), 217–52.

28. Hannah Arendt, "Introduction: Walter Benjamin, 1892–1940," in Benjamin, *Illuminations*, 2.

29. I'm using here the triadic semiotics of Charles Sanders Peirce because of the way it formalizes the phenomenology of indexical experience in Adorno's description. Peirce describes the *hic et nunc* ("here and now") of indexical experience that arise through his phenomenological category of "secondness." However, there are of course other senses of indexicality. See Jeffrey R. Di Leo, "The Semiotics of Indexical Experience," in *Semiotics 1989*, eds. John Deely, Karen Haworth, and Terry Prewitt (Lantham, MD: University Press of America, 1990), 10–15, for an overview of Peirce's work here.

30. Theodor W. Adorno, "Radio Physiognomics," in *Current of Music*, 36.

31. Adorno, "Curves of the Needle," 50.

32. Ibid., 50.

33. Ibid., 51.

34. Ibid., 51.

35. Ibid., 52.

36. Ibid., 54.
37. Ibid., 54.
38. Ibid., 54. It should also be noted that early phonographs could both record sound as well as play it back.
39. Jacques Lacan, "The Mirror Stage as Formative of the *I* Function, as Revealed in Psychoanalytic Experience," in *Écrits: A Selection*, trans. Bruce Fink (1949; New York: Norton, 2002), 3–9.
40. Calvin Thomas, "Mirror Stage," in *The Bloomsbury Handbook of Literary and Cultural Theory*, ed. Jeffrey R. Di Leo (London: Bloomsbury, 2019), 577.
41. Adorno, "Curves of the Needle," 54.
42. Ibid., 54.
43. Ibid., 54.
44. Ibid., 54.
45. Ibid., 54.
46. Ibid., 54.
47. Ibid., 54.
48. Ibid., 55.
49. Ibid., 55.
50. Theodor W. Adorno, "Die Form der Schallplatte," *23: Eine Wiener Musikzeitschrift* 17–19 (December 15, 1934): 35–39.
51. Levin, "For the Record," 31n20.
52. Adorno also published his controversial essay "Über Jazz" under the same pseudonym, albeit in a different journal, *Zeitschrift für Sozialforschung* 5 (1936): 235–59.
53. Theodor W. Adorno, "The Form of the Phonograph Record," trans. Thomas Y. Levin, *October* 55 (Winter 1990): 57.
54. Ibid., 58.
55. Ibid., 57.
56. Ibid., 57.
57. Ibid., 57n3.
58. See "Player piano," https://www.britannica.com/art/player-piano.
59. Igor Stravinsky, "Meine Stellung zur Schallplatte," *Kulture und Schallplatte* 1 (1930). Cited and translated by Thomas Y. Levin in Adorno, "Form of the Phonograph Record," 57n3.
60. Adorno, "Form of the Phonograph Record," 58.
61. Ibid., 56.
62. Ibid., 56.
63. Ibid., 58.
64. Ibid., 58.

65. Ibid., 58.

66. Ibid., 56.

67. Ibid., 59.

68. Ibid., 59. Here Adorno is quoting Walter Benjamin, *The Origin of German Tragic Drama* (1928), his habilitation for the University of Frankfurt in 1925. It was submitted to the university by Benjamin but later withdrawn.

69. Ibid., 59.

70. Ibid., 59.

71. Theodor W. Adorno, "'Die Oper überwintert auf der Langspielplatte': Theodor W. Adorno über die Revolution der Schallplatte," *Der Spiegel,* March 24, 1969, 169.

72. Theodor W. Adorno, "Opera and the Long-Playing Record," trans. Thomas Y. Levin, *October* 55 (Winter 1990): 63.

73. Chanan, *Repeated Takes*, 66.

74. Ibid., 93. It should also be noted that the 45 rpm record was introduced by RCA Victor in 1949, a technology that unlike the 33 1/3 LP would not be immune to Adorno's early criticisms of the phonographic record.

75. Adorno, "Opera and the Long-Playing Record," 63.

76. Ibid., 63.

77. Chanan, *Repeated Takes*, 92.

78. Adorno, "Opera and the Long-Playing Record," 64.

79. Ibid., 64.

80. Ibid., 65.

81. Ibid., 65.

82. Ibid., 65.

83. Ibid., 62.

84. Ibid., 66.

85. Ibid., 65.

86. Theodor W. Adorno, *Introduction to the Sociology of Music*, trans. E. B. Ashton (New York: Seabury Press, 1976), 134. English translation of *Einleitung in die Musiksoziologie: Zwölf theoretische Vorlesungen* (Frankfurt am Main: Suhrkamp Verlag, 1962).

87. Adorno, *Introduction*, 134.

88. Adorno, "Radio Physiognomics," 75.

89. Adorno, *Introduction*, 134.

90. Ibid., 135.

91. Ibid., 135.

92. Starting in the 1950s, polyvinyl chloride became a common material in record production. Thus, the term *vinyl* came to be short for "vinyl phonographic records."

CHAPTER THREE

1. The first commercially available vinyl long-playing records were produced by RCA in 1931. See Mike Evans, *Vinyl: The Art of Making Records* (New York: Sterling, 2015), 34.

2. See Georges Dumézil, *Mythe et épopée* (Paris: Gallimard, 1968). Cited by Attali, *Noise*, 87.

3. Plato, *Theaetetus*, trans. F. M. Cornford, in *The Complete Dialogues of Plato*, eds. Edith Hamilton and Huntington Cairns (Princeton, NJ: Princeton University Press, 1961), 191d.

4. Ibid., 191e.

5. Ibid., 194c; Homer, *Iliad* 2.851; 16.554.

6. One of the major questions of Plato's *Theaetetus* is whether knowledge is justified true belief. While the term *knowledge* is used here, its relationship with others such as "information," "belief," and "fact" will be bracketed. Still, these epistemological questions are important ones even with respect to vinyl records, where the relationship between the "original" sound and its "recording" are the subject of varying positions.

7. Cormac Ó Gráda, *Famine: A Short History* (Princeton, NJ: Princeton University Press, 2009), 32.

8. Ibid., 229.

9. Ibid., 229.

10. Attali, *Noise*, 87; my emphasis.

11. Ibid., 87.

12. Ibid., 87.

13. Ibid., 87.

14. See Adorno, *Current of Music*.

15. Ibid., 77.

16. Ibid., 90.

17. Evans, *Vinyl*, 72.

18. "Which is which?" Victor Talking Machine advertisement, 1908 in Jonathan Sterne, *The Audible Past: Cultural Origins of Sound Reproduction* (Durham, NC: Duke University Press, 2003), 217.

19. CPI Inflation Calculator, http://www.in2013dollars.com.

20. Sterne, *Audible Past*, 216.

21. "The human voice *is* human," Victor Victrola advertisement, March 3, 1927.

22. Adorno, "Curves of the Needle," 52.

23. Ibid., 49.

24. Ibid., 49.

25. Sterne, *Audible Past*, 219.

26. Ibid., 219.
27. Ibid., 219.
28. Ibid., 221.
29. Ibid., 221.
30. Sarah Thornton, *Club Cultures: Music, Media, and Subcultural Capital* (Middletown, CT: Wesleyan University Press, 1996), 42–43, quoted in Sterne, *Audible Past*, 221.
31. Sterne, *Audible Past*, 222.
32. Michel Chion, *Sound: An Acoulogical Treatise,* trans. James A. Steintrager (Durham, NC: Duke University Press, 2016), 133–41.
33. Ibid., 141.
34. Ibid., 141.
35. Ibid., 141.
36. Eugene Holland, "Studies in Applied Nomadology: Jazz Improvisation and Post-Capitalist Markets," in *Deleuze and Music*, eds. Ian Buchanan and Marcel Swiboda (Edinburgh: Edinburgh University Press, 2004), 28.
37. René Girard, *La Violence et le sacré* (Paris: Bernard Grasset, 1972).
38. Catherine Bell, *Ritual Theory, Ritual Practice* (New York: Oxford University Press, 1992), 173.
39. Ibid., 173.
40. Ibid., 173.
41. Holland, "Studies in Applied Nomadology," 29.
42. Spike Lee with Lisa Jones, *Do the Right Thing: A Spike Lee Joint* (New York: Fireside, 1989), 24.
43. "Fight the Power" was released as a single in June of 1989 on Motown Records. It was conceived by Public Enemy at the request of Spike Lee, who requested it as theme music for *Do the Right Thing*. It is also found on the 1989 original film soundtrack. A different version is found on Public Enemy's studio album *Fear of a Black Planet* (1990).
44. Lee with Jones, *Do the Right Thing*, 208. All dialogue from the film comes from the script published in the companion volume, which is listed as the "Second Draft, March 1, 1998 (WGA #45816)."
45. Ibid., 164.
46. Ibid., 164.
47. Ibid., 192.
48. Ibid., 193.
49. Ibid., 239.
50. Ibid., 237.
51. Ibid., 238.

52. Ibid., 241.

53. Ibid., 242–43.

54. Ibid., 243–44.

55. Ibid., 113.

56. Ibid., 114.

57. Ibid., 25.

58. Ibid., 121.

59. Ibid., 121.

60. Ibid., 121.

61. Ibid., 122.

62. Ibid., 121.

63. Ibid., 122.

64. Roger Ebert, "Do the Right Thing," rogerebert.com, May 27, 2001, www.rogerebert.com/reviews/great-movie-do-the-right-thing-1989.

65. Janice Simpson, "Music: Yo! Rap Gets on the Map," *Time,* February 5, 1990, 60.

66. Attali, *Noise,* 122.

67. Ibid., 122.

68. *The Epic of the Gilgamesh,* trans. N. K. Sanders (Harmondsworth, UK: Penguin, 1971), 105; quoted in R. Murray Schafer, *The Soundscape: Our Sonic Environment and the Tuning of the World* (1977; Rochester, VT: Destiny Books, 1994), 189.

69. Schafer, *Soundscape,* 189.

70. Ibid., 190.

71. Lee with Jones, *Do the Right Thing,* 121.

72. Ibid., 122.

CHAPTER FOUR

1. John Atkins, *The Who on Record: A Critical History, 1963–1998* (Jefferson, NC: McFarland, 2000), 97.

2. The image is of the first pressing of *We're Only in It for the Money* from 1968 with the original insert. Zappa thought that the gatefold should have been the front and back covers of the album, but the record company made them reverse the images. Also, the record company made them alter the music and the lyrics too. Zappa turned down an award for the album saying that it should instead be given to whomever did the changes to the album jacket, lyrics, and music. Later it was released as originally intended but only after Zappa achieved complete control over his material and label.

3. The larger project included the three other albums, *Lumpy Gravy* (1967), *Uncle Meat* (1969), and *Cruising with Ruben & the Jets* (1968), in addition to *We're Only in It for the Money* (1968). In his 1968 *Rolling Stone* interview with Jerry Hopkins, Zappa said, "It's all one album. All the material in the albums is organically related and if I had all the master tapes and I could take a razor blade and cut them apart and put it together again in a different order it still would make one piece of music you can listen to. Then I could take that razor blade and cut it apart and reassemble it a different way, and it still would make sense. I could do this twenty ways. The material is definitely related" (Jerry Hopkins, "The Rolling Stone Interview: Frank Zappa," *Rolling Stone,* July 20, 1968).

4. Interestingly, the title of the Beatles' fourth album, *Beatles for Sale* (1964), is even more direct as to the ends of the band. Recorded at the height of their fame, this album title draws attention to the fact that in 1964 they were being sold in every way possible: not only did they record and release two new albums as well as an EP in 1964, they also starred in their first feature film (*A Hard Day's Night*), appeared on radio and television, and were on world tour.

5. See David Fricke's liner notes to *The Lumpy Money Project/Object*. This is a compilation album of two Mothers of Invention/Frank Zappa albums, *Lumpy Gravy* (1967) and *We're Only in It for the Money* (1968), released by Zappa (Records) on January 23, 2009.

6. Atkins, *The Who on Record,* 20.

7. Ibid., 21.

8. Ibid., 20.

9. Ibid., 5.

10. All album date releases for The Who come from Atkins, *The Who on Record*, "Appendix 1," 281-288.

11. Ibid., 22.

12. Ibid., 78.

13. Ibid., 76.

14. Ibid., 92.

15. Ben Toney, "The Amazing Radio London Adventure," n.d., http://www.radiolondon.co.uk/rl/bentoney/book.html. Accessed February 28, 2019.

16. Ibid.

17. Ibid.

18. Ibid.

19. See ibid. for a wonderful overview of Radio London from its origins to its end including many of its colorful stories.

20. Given that Radio London and other pirate radio stations were shut down

in August 1967, and the album was released in December of 1967, the Who's album is both a satire of these stations as well a kind of homage to their loss.

21. Atkins, *The Who on Record*, 94.

22. Quoted in Atkins, *The Who on Record*, 87.

23. Quoted in Atkins, *The Who on Record*, 88.

24. Richard Barnes and Pete Townshend, *The Story of Tommy* (Middlesex, UK: Eel Pie Publishing, 1977). Quoted in Atkins, *The Who on Record*, 88.

25. Unlike the Who, the relationship of Frank Zappa to the music industry is a long and complex story that cannot be reduced to one album. See Ben Watson, *Frank Zappa: The Negative Dialectics of Poodle Play* (New York: St. Martin's, 1993), for a comprehensive survey of Zappa's recording career.

26. Richard Green, "Who's Sick Opera," *New Musical Express*, May 24, 1969. Cited in Atkins, *The Who on Record*, 126.

27. Barry Miles, "Review of The Who's *Tommy*," *It*, May 9–22, 1969. Cited in Atkins, *The Who on Record*, 126.

28. To clarify, Derrida first employed the rhetoric of *deconstruction* in "Writing Before the Letter," a review article published in the Parisian journal *Critique* in December 1965 and January 1966. However, three works from 1967 definitively established the full force of the term: *Speech and Phenomena, Of Grammatology,* and *Writing and Difference*. See Benoît Peeters, *Derrida: A Biography* (Cambridge, UK: Polity, 2013), 159–60; and Henry Sussman, "Deconstruction," in *The Bloomsbury Handbook of Literary and Cultural Theory*, ed. Jeffrey R. Di Leo (London: Bloomsbury, 2019), 112–24.

29. For an excellent account of Frank Zappa's critique of the music industry, see Watson, *Frank Zappa*.

30. "Sell out," *Urban Dictionary*, proposed August 3, 2003, by Sean Piece, https://www.urbandictionary.com/define.php?term=sell%20out&amp=true.

31. As determined from some of the more popular entries for "sell out" in the Urban Dictionary.

32. See Jeffrey R. Di Leo, "There Is No Success Like Failure," *American Book Review* 35, no. 4 (2014), for a reading of Dylan's performance at Newport.

33. For an excellent, albeit controversial, account of the rise of vocationalism in higher education, see Andrew Hacker and Claudia Dreifus, *Higher Education? How Colleges Are Wasting Our Money and Failing Our Kids—and What We Can Do about It* (New York: Times Books/Henry Holt, 2010). For a critique of higher education's vocational telos, see Jeffrey R. Di Leo, *Corporate Humanities in Higher Education: Moving beyond the Neoliberal Academy* (New York: Palgrave Macmillan, 2013).

34. Helen Davies with Terry Eagleton, "A Theoretical Blow for Democracy,"

Times Higher Education, June 1, 2001. https://www.timeshighereducation. com/news/a-theoretical-blow-for-democracy/160508.article.

35. Paul Vallely, "Terry Eagleton: Class Warrior," *The Independent,* October 13, 2007, https://www.independent.co.uk/news/people/profiles/terry-eagle- ton-class-warrior-396770.html.

36. Terry Eagleton, *The Gatekeeper: A Memoir* (New York: St. Martin's, 2001), 71.

37. Davies with Eagleton, "Theoretical Blow."

38. Vallely, "Terry Eagleton."

39. Terry Eagleton, *Literary Theory: An Introduction* (Minneapolis: University of Minnesota Press, 1983), vii.

41. William Deresiewicz, "The Business of Theory," *The Nation,* January 29, 2004, https://www.thenation.com/article/business-theory/.

42. Lorenzo Perez, "UVA English Professor Lands Large Danish Grant to Explore Literature's Social Use," *UVA Today,* May 25, 2016, https://news.virginia.edu/ content/uva-english-professor-lands-large-danish-grant-explore-literatures- social-use.

45. Eagleton, *Literary Theory*, vii.

46. The notion of the docile subjects of neoliberal academe is established in some depth in Di Leo, *Corporate Humanities*. Two of the major theses of the book are (1) neoliberalism threatens to turn academics into docile subjects (xvii- xviii), and (2) docile academic subjects are a bad thing (xviii–xix).

47. Jonathan Kramnick, "English by the Grim Numbers," *Chronicle of Higher Edu- cation,* January 25, 2019, B5.

Bibliography

Adorno, Theodor W. *Current of Music: Elements of a Radio Theory*. Edited by Robert Hullot-Kentor. Malden, MA: Polity, 2009.

Adorno, Theodor W. "The Curves of the Needle." Translated by Thomas Y. Levin. *October* 55 (Winter 1990): 48–55.

Adorno, Theodor W. "Die Form der Schallplatte." *23: Eine Wiener Musikzeitschrift* 17–19 (December 15, 1934): 35–39. Signed "Hektor Rottweiler."

Adorno, Theodor W. "'Die Oper überwintert auf der Langspielplatte': Theodor W. Adorno über die Revolution der Schallplatte." *Der Spiegel,* March 24, 1969, 169. https://magazin.spiegel.de/EpubDelivery/spiegel/pdf/45702462.

Adorno, Theodor W. *Einleitung in die Musiksoziologie: Zwölf Theoretische Vorlesungen*. Frankfurt am Main: Suhrkamp Verlag, 1962.

Adorno, Theodor W. "The Form of the Phonograph Record." Translated by Thomas Y. Levin. *October* 55 (Winter 1990): 56–61.

Adorno, Theodor W. *Introduction to the Sociology of Music*. 1962. Translated by E. B. Ashton. New York: Seabury Press, 1976.

Adorno, Theodor W. *Minima Moralia: Reflections from Damaged Life*. 1951. Translated by E. F. N. Jephcott. London: Verso, 1994.

Adorno, Theodor W. "Nadelkurven." *Musikblätter des Anbruch* 10 (February 1928): 47–50.

Adorno, Theodor W. "Nadelkurven." *Phono: Internationale Schallplatten-Zeitschrift* 6 (July–August 1965): 123–24.

Adorno, Theodor W. "On Popular Music [With the assistance of George Simpson]." 1941. In *Essays on Music: Selected, with Introduction, Commentary, and Notes*, by Theodor W. Adorno, edited by Richard Leppert, 437–69. Berkeley: University of California Press, 2002.

Adorno, Theodor W. "Opera and the Long-Playing Record." Translated by Thomas Y. Levin. *October* 55 (Winter 1990): 62–66.

Adorno, Theodor W. *Philosophy of Modern Music.* 1949. Translated by Anne G. Mitchell and Wesley V. Blomster. New York: The Seabury Press, 1973.

Adorno, Theodor W. "Radio Physiognomics." 1940. In *Current of Music: Elements of a Radio Theory,* by Theodor W. Adorno, edited by Robert Hullot-Kentor, 41–132. Malden, MA: Polity, 2009.

Adorno, Theodor W. "The Radio Voice." 1939. In *Current of Music: Elements of a Radio Theory,* edited by Robert Hullot-Kentor, 345–91. Malden, MA: Polity, 2009.

Adorno, Theodor W. "Über Jazz." *Zeitschrift für Sozialforschung* 5 (1936): 235–59. Signed "Hektor Rottweiler."

Adorno, Theodor W. "Zum *Anbruch*: Exposé." In *Musikalische Schriften VI,* edited by Rolf Tiedemann, 601–2. Vol. 19 of *Gesammelte Schriften.* Frankfurt am Main: Suhrkamp, 1984.

Adorno, Theodor W. "Zum Jahrgang 1929 des *Anbruch*." In *Musikalische Schriften VI,* edited by Rolf Tiedemann, 605–8. Vol. 19 of *Gesammelte Schriften.* Frankfurt am Main: Suhrkamp, 1984.

Arendt, Hannah. "Introduction: Walter Benjamin, 1892–1940." In *Illuminations,* by Walter Benjamin, edited by Hannah Arendt, translated by Harry Zohn, 1–58. New York: Schocken Books, 1968.

Atkins, John. *The Who on Record: A Critical History, 1963–1998.* Jefferson, NC: McFarland, 2000.

Attali, Jacques. *After the Crisis: How Did This Happen?* Portland, OR: Eska Publishing, 2010.

Attali, Jacques. *Analyse économique de la vie politique.* Paris: Presses Universitaires de France, 1972.

Attali, Jacques. *A Brief History of the Future: A Brave and Controversial Look at the Twenty-First Century.* Translated by Jeremy Leggatt. New York: Arcade Publishing, 2009.

Attali, Jacques. *Bruits: Essai sur l'économie politique de la musique.* Paris: Presses Universitaires de France, 1977.

Attali, Jacques. *The Economic History of the Jewish People.* Foreword by Alan Dershowitz. Portland, OR: Eska Publishing, 2010.

Attali, Jacques. *From Crystal to Smoke.* Portland, OR: Eska Publishing, 2010.

Attali, Jacques. *The Labyrinth in Culture and Society: Pathways to Wisdom.* Translated by Joseph Rowe. Berkeley, CA: North Atlantic Books, 1998.

Attali, Jacques. *La nouvelle économie française.* Paris: Flammarion, 1978.

Attali, Jacques. *La parole et l'outil.* Paris: Presses Universitaires de France, 1975.

Attali, Jacques. *Les modèles politiques.* Paris: Presses Universitaires de France, 1972.

Attali, Jacques. *Les trois mondes.* Paris: Fayard, 1981.

Attali, Jacques. *L'ordre cannibale: Vie et mort de la médicine.* Paris: Grasset, 1979.

Attali, Jacques. *A Man of Influence: The Extraordinary Career of S. G. Warburg.* Translated by Barbara Ellis. Bethesda, MD: Adler & Adler, 1987.

Attali, Jacques. *Millennium: Winners and Losers in the Coming World Order.* Translated by Leila Conners and Nathan Gardels. New York: Times Books, 1991.

Attali, Jacques. *Noise: The Political Economy of Music.* Translated by Brian Massumi. Minneapolis: University of Minnesota Press, 1985.

Barnes, Richard, and Pete Townshend. *The Story of Tommy.* Middlesex, UK: Eel Pie Publishing, 1977.

Barth, John. "The Literature of Exhaustion." 1967. In *The Friday Book: Essays and Other Nonfiction,* 62–76. Baltimore, MD: Johns Hopkins University Press, 1984.

Barthes, Roland. "The Death of the Author." 1967. In *Image Music Text,* edited and translated by Stephen Heath, 142–48. New York: Hill and Wang, 1977.

Beatles, The. *Beatles for Sale.* UK LP. Parlophone (PC 1240) [mono]/(PCS 3062) [stereo]. Released December 4, 1964.

Beatles, The. *Meet the Beatles.* US LP. Capitol (T 2047) [mono]/(ST 2047) [stereo]. Released January 20, 1964.

Beatles, The. *Rubber Soul.* US LP. Capitol (T 2442) [mono]/(ST 2442) [stereo]. Released December 6, 1965.

Beatles, The. *Sgt. Pepper's Lonely Hearts Club Band.* US LP. Capitol (MAS 2653) [mono]/(SMAS 2653) [stereo]. Released June 2, 1967. Fiftieth anniversary edition. Capitol (B0027772-01) [stereo/180 gram]. Released December 15, 2017.

Bell, Catherine. *Ritual Theory, Ritual Practice.* New York: Oxford University Press, 1992.

Benjamin, Walter. *The Origin of German Tragic Drama.* 1928. Translated by John Osborne. London: Verso, 2009.

Benjamin, Walter. "The Work of Art in the Age of Mechanical Reproduction." 1936. In *Illuminations,* by Walter Benjamin, edited by Hannah Arendt, translated by Harry Zohn, 217–52. New York: Schocken Books, 1968.

Berg, Alban, and Arnold Schoenberg. *The Berg-Schoenberg Correspondence: Selected Letters.* Edited by Juliane Brand, Christopher Hailey, and Donald Harris. Translated by Juliane Brand and Christopher Hailey. New York: Norton, 1987.

Blackmore, Jason, dir. *Records Collecting Dust.* Documentary. Riot House Pictures, 2015.

Broadway, Jeff, dir. *Our Vinyl Weighs a Ton: This Is Stones Throw Records.* Documentary. Gatling Pictures, 2013.

Boston, John, dir. *Re-Vinylized.* Documentary. Whiskey Bender Productions, 2011.

Buchanan, Ian. "Introduction: Deleuze and Music." In *Deleuze and Music*, edited by Ian Buchanan and Marcel Swiboda, 1–20. Edinburgh: Edinburgh University Press, 2004.

Campana, Paolo, dir. *Vinylmania: When Life Runs at 33 Revolutions per Minute.* Documentary. Stetfilm and ZDF in co-production with Lato Sensu Productions, in collaboration with ARTE, in association with YLE Teema, MDR, 2012.

Chanan, Michael. *Repeated Takes: A Short History of Recording and Its Effects on Music.* London: Verso, 1995.

Chion, Michel. *Sound: An Acoulogical Treatise.* Translated by James A. Steintrager. Durham, NC: Duke University Press, 2016.

Christmas with the Chipmunks. US LP. Liberty (LRP 3256) [mono]. Released 1962.

Cooper, Alice. *Alice Cooper Goes to Hell.* US LP. Warner Bros. (BS 2896). Released 1976.

Davies, Helen, with Terry Eagleton. "A Theoretical Blow for Democracy." *Times Higher Education,* June 1, 2001. https://www.timeshighereducation.com/news/a-theoretical-blow-for-democracy/160508.article.

Davis, Miles, with Quincy Troupe. *Miles: The Autobiography.* New York: Simon and Schuster, 1989.

Deleuze, Gilles, and Félix Guattari. *A Thousand Plateaus: Capitalism and Schizophrenia.* Translated by Brian Massumi. Minneapolis: University of Minnesota Press, 1987. Translation of *Capitalisme et Schizophrénie.* Vol. 2. Paris: Les Editions de Minuit, 1980.

Deresiewicz, William. "The Business of Theory." *The Nation,* January 29, 2004. https://www.thenation.com/article/business-theory/.

Derrida, Jacques. *Of Grammatology.* 1967. Translated by Gayatri Chakravorty Spivak. Baltimore, MD: Johns Hopkins University Press, 1976.

Derrida, Jacques. *Speech and Phenomena.* 1967. Translated by David B. Allison. Evanston, IL: Northwestern University Press, 1973.

Derrida, Jacques. *Writing and Difference.* 1967. Translated by Alan Bass. Chicago: University of Chicago Press, 1978.

Deutsch, Otto Erich. *Mozart: A Documentary Biography.* Stanford: Stanford University Press, 1965.

Di Leo, Jeffrey R. *Corporate Humanities in Higher Education: Moving beyond the Neoliberal Academy.* New York: Palgrave Macmillan, 2013.

Di Leo, Jeffrey R. *The End of American Literature: Essays from the Late Age of Print.* Huntsville, TX: Texas Review Press, 2019.

Di Leo, Jeffrey R. Review of Friedrich A. Kittler, *Gramophone, Film, Typewriter* (1999). *The Comparatist* 25 (2001): 176–78.

Di Leo, Jeffrey R. "The Semiotics of Indexical Experience." In *Semiotics 1989*, edited by John Deely, Karen Haworth, and Terry Prewitt, 10–15. Lantham, MD: University Press of America, 1990.

Di Leo, Jeffrey R. "There Is No Success Like Failure." *American Book Review* 35, no. 4 (2014): 2, 24.

Di Leo, Jeffrey R. *Turning the Page: Book Culture in the Digital Age.* Huntsville, TX: Texas Review Press, 2014.

Doctor Dolittle. US LP. Original soundtrack. 20th Century Fox Records (DTC 5101) [mono]/(DTCS 5101) [stereo]. Released September 1967.

Dumézil, Georges. *Mythe et épopée.* Paris: Gallimard, 1968.

Dylan, Bob. *Greatest Hits.* US LP. Columbia (KCL 2663) [mono]/(KCS 9463) [stereo]. Released March 27, 1967.

Eagleton, Terry. *After Theory.* New York: Basic Books, 2003.

Eagleton, Terry. *The Gatekeeper: A Memoir.* New York: St. Martin's, 2001.

Eagleton, Terry. *Literary Theory: An Introduction.* Minneapolis: University of Minnesota Press, 1983. Anniversary edition with a new preface. Minneapolis: University of Minnesota Press, 2008.

Easy Rider. US LP. Original soundtrack of the film. ABC/Dunhill Records (DSX 50063). Released 1969.

Ebert, Roger. "Do the Right Thing." rogerebert.com, May 27, 2001, https://www.rogerebert.com/reviews/great-movie-do-the-right-thing-1989.

The Epic of the Gilgamesh. Translated by N. K. Sanders. Harmondsworth, UK: Penguin, 1971.

Evans, Mike. *Vinyl: The Art of Making Records.* New York: Sterling, 2015.

Finlay, Jeanie, dir. *Sound It Out.* Documentary. Glimmer Films, 2011.

Foucault, Michel. *The Birth of Biopolitics: Lectures at the Collège de France, 1978–1979.* Edited by Michael Senellart. Translated by Braham Burchell. New York: Picador/Palgrave Macmillan, 2008.

Foucault, Michel. *The History of Sexuality: Volume I: An Introduction.* Translated by Robert Hurley. New York: Pantheon, 1978. Translation of *La volonté de savoir.* Paris: Editions Gallimard, 1976.

Foucault, Michel. *Security, Territory, Population: Lectures at the Collège de France, 1977–1978.* Edited by Michael Senellart. Translated by Braham Burchell. New York: Picador/Palgrave Macmillan, 2007.

Foucault, Michel. *"Society Must Be Defended": Lectures at the Collège de France, 1975–1976.* Edited by Mauro Bertani and Alessandro Fontana. Translated by David Macey. New York: Picador/Palgrave Macmillan, 2003.

Gillan, Edward, dir. *Desperate Man Blues: Discovering the Roots of American Music.* Documentary. BBC4, 2003.

Girard, René. *La Violence et le sacré*. Paris: Bernard Grasset, 1972.

Gordon, Peter E., and Alexander Rehding. "Editors' Introduction: Adorno, Music, Modernity." *New German Critique* 43, no. 3 (2016): 1–4.

Green, Richard. "Who's Sick Opera." *New Musical Express*, May 24, 1969.

Hacker, Andrew, and Claudia Dreifus. *Higher Education? How Colleges Are Wasting Our Money and Failing Our Kids—and What We Can Do about It*. New York: Times Books/Henry Holt, 2010.

Hanks, Colin, dir. *All Things Must Pass: The Rise and Fall of Tower Records*. Documentary. Gravitas Ventures/Company Name, 2015.

Holland, Eugene. "Studies in Applied Nomadology: Jazz Improvisation and Post-Capitalist Markets." In *Deleuze and Music*, edited by Ian Buchanan and Marcel Swiboda, 20–35. Edinburgh: Edinburgh University Press, 2004.

Hopkins, Jerry. "The Rolling Stone Interview: Frank Zappa." *Rolling Stone*, July 20, 1968. https://www.rollingstone.com/music/music-news/the-rolling-stone-interview-frank-zappa-81967/.

Horkheimer, Max, and Theodor W. Adorno. "The Culture Industry: Enlightenment as Mass Deception." 1944. In *Dialectic of Enlightenment: Philosophical Fragments*, translated by John Cumming, 120–67. New York: Seabury Press, 1972. Originally published as *Philosophische fragmente*. New York: Social Studies Association, Inc., 1944.

Humperdinck, Engelbert. US LP. *After the Lovin'*. Epic/MAM (PE 34381). Released 1976.

Jameson, Fredric. Foreword to *Noise: The Political Economy of Music*, by Jacques Attali, vii–xiv. Translated by Brian Massumi. Minneapolis: University of Minnesota Press, 1985.

Joplin, Janis. *Pearl*. US LP. Columbia (KC30322). Released January 11, 1971.

Khanna, Vish. "Why Aren't There More Vinyl Pressing Plants?" *Pitchfork*, June 9, 2014. https://pitchfork.com/thepitch/363-why-arent-there-more-vinyl-pressing-plants/amp/.

Kirkley, Christine, prod. *Red Beans and Rice*. Documentary. Jamille Records, 2010.

KISS. *Rock and Roll Over*. US LP. Casablanca (NBLP 7037). Released November 11, 1976.

Kittler, Friedrich A. *Gramophone, Film, Typewriter*. Translated by Geoffrey Winthrop-Young and Michael Wutz. Stanford, CA: Stanford University Press, 1999.

Kramnick, Jonathan. "English by the Grim Numbers." *Chronicle of Higher Education*, January 25, 2019, B4–B5.

Lacan, Jacques. "The Mirror Stage as Formative of the *I* Function, as Revealed in Psychoanalytic Experience." 1949. In *Écrits: A Selection*, translated by Bruce Fink, 3–9. New York: Norton, 2002.

Led Zeppelin. *Led Zeppelin.* US LP. Atlantic (SD 8216). Released January 12, 1969.

Lee, Spike, with Lisa Jones. *Do the Right Thing: A Spike Lee Joint.* New York: Fireside, 1989.

Leibowitz, René. *Schoenberg and His School: The Contemporary Stage of the Language of Music.* Translated by Dika Newlin. New York: Philosophical Library, 1949.

Leppert, Richard. "Commentary." In *Essays on Music: Selected, with Introduction, Commentary, and Notes,* by Theodor W. Adorno, edited by Richard Leppert, 213–50. Berkeley: University of California Press, 2002.

Leppert, Richard. Introduction to *Essays on Music: Selected, with Introduction, Commentary, and Notes,* by Theodor W. Adorno, 1–84. Edited by Richard Leppert. Berkeley: University of California Press, 2002.

Levin, Thomas Y. "For the Record: Adorno on Music in the Age of Its Technological Reproducibility." *October* 55 (Winter 1990): 23–47.

Liese, Andrea. "Food Security." In *The Oxford Handbook of Governance and Limited Statehood,* edited by Thomas Risse, Tanja A. Börzel, and Anke Draude, 459–78. Oxford: Oxford University Press, 2018.

Massumi, Brian. *Politics of Affect.* Malden, MA: Polity, 2015.

Miles, Barry. "Review of The Who's *Tommy.*" *It,* May 9–22, 1969.

Morris, Chris. "As Vinyl Surges, a Boutique Pressing Plant Helps Smaller Indies Get an In." *Variety,* April 23, 2018. https://variety.com/2018/music/news/vinyl-record-pressing-plant-fills-lp-niche-1202784124/.

Nietzsche, Friedrich. *The Case of Wagner.* In *The Birth of Tragedy and The Case of Wagner,* translated by Walter Kaufman, 153–92. New York: Vintage, 1967.

Nietzsche, Friedrich. *Ecce Homo.* In *On the Genealogy of Morals and Ecce Homo,* translated by Walter Kaufman, 197–344. New York: Vintage, 1969.

Nietzsche, Friedrich. *The Gay Science.* Translated by Walter Kaufmann. New York: Vintage, 1974.

Nietzsche, Friedrich. *Nietzsche contra Wagner.* In *The Portable Nietzsche,* edited and translated by Walter Kaufmann, 661–83. New York: Viking, 1954.

Nietzsche, Friedrich. *Twilight of the Idols, or How One Philosophizes with a Hammer.* In *The Portable Nietzsche,* edited and translated by Walter Kaufmann, 463–563. New York: Viking, 1954.

Ó Gráda, Cormac. *Famine: A Short History.* Princeton, NJ: Princeton University Press, 2009.

O'Hagan, Steve, dir. *When Albums Ruled the World.* Documentary. BBC, 2013.

Paddison, Max. "The Critique Criticised: Adorno and Popular Music." *Popular Music* 2 (1982): 201–18.

Peeters, Benoît. *Derrida: A Biography.* Cambridge, UK: Polity, 2013.

Perez, Lorenzo. "UVA English Professor Lands Large Danish Grant to Explore Literature's Social Use." *UVA Today,* May 25, 2016. https://news.virginia.edu/content/uva-english-professor-lands-large-danish-grant-explore-literatures-social-use.

Piper, Pip, dir. *Last Shop Standing: The Rise, Fall and Rebirth of the Independent Record Shop.* Documentary. Blue Hippo Media, 2012.

Plato. *Theaetetus.* Translated by F. M. Cornford. In *The Complete Dialogues of Plato,* edited by Edith Hamilton and Huntington Cairns, 845–919. Princeton, NJ: Princeton University Press, 1961.

Pray, Doug, dir. *Scratch.* Documentary. Palm Pictures/Ridgeway Entertainment, 2001.

Rorty, Richard. *The Linguistic Turn: Recent Essays in Philosophical Method.* Chicago: University of Chicago Press, 1967.

Schafer, R. Murray. *The Soundscape: Our Sonic Environment and the Tuning of the World.* Rochester, VT: Destiny Books, 1994. Originally published as *Tuning of the World.* New York: Knopf, 1977.

Shepherd, Elaine, dir. *John Peel's Record Box.* Documentary. Endemol UK pic/Channel 4 Television Corporation MMV, 2005.

Shklovsky, Viktor. "Art, as Device." Translated by Alexandra Berlina. *Poetics Today* 36, no. 3 (2015): 151–74.

Simpson, Janice. "Music: Yo! Rap Gets on the Map." *Time,* February 5, 1990.

Sterne, Jonathan. *The Audible Past: Cultural Origins of Sound Reproduction.* Durham, NC: Duke University Press, 2003.

Stravinsky, Igor. *An Autobiography.* 1936. New York: Norton, 1962.

Stravinsky, Igor. "Meine Stellung zur Schallplatte." *Kulture und Schallplatte* 1 (March 1930): 65.

Steve Miller Band. US LP. *Fly Like an Eagle.* Capitol (ST-11497). Released 1976.

Sussman, Henry. "Deconstruction." In *The Bloomsbury Handbook of Literary and Cultural Theory,* edited by Jeffrey R. Di Leo, 112–24. London: Bloomsbury, 2019.

Thomas, Calvin. "Mirror Stage." In *The Bloomsbury Handbook of Literary and Cultural Theory,* edited by Jeffrey R. Di Leo, 576–77. London: Bloomsbury, 2019.

Thornton, Sarah. *Club Cultures: Music, Media, and Subcultural Capital.* Middletown, CT: Wesleyan University Press, 1996.

Toller, Brendan, dir. *I Need That Record! The Death (or Possible Survival) of the Independent Record Store.* Documentary. Unsatisfied Films, 2008.

Toney, Ben. "The Amazing Radio London Adventure." n.d. http://www.radiolondon.co.uk/rl/bentoney/book.html. Accessed February 28, 2019.

"2017 U.S. Music Year-End Report." *Nielsen,* January 3, 2018. https://www.nielsen.com/us/en/insights/report/2018/2017-music-us-year-end-report/.

Vallely, Paul. "Terry Eagleton: Class Warrior." *The Independent,* October 13, 2007. https://www.independent.co.uk/news/people/profiles/terry-eagleton-class-warrior-396770.html.

Watson, Ben. *Frank Zappa: The Negative Dialectics of Poodle Play.* New York: St. Martin's, 1993.

Who, The. *Happy Jack.* US LP. Decca (DL 4892) [mono]/(DL 74892) [stereo]. Released May 1967.

Who, The. *My Generation.* UK LP. Brunswick (LAT 8618) [mono]. Released December 4, 1965.

Who, The. *A Quick One.* UK LP. Reaction (593 002) [mono]. Released December 3, 1966.

Who, The. *Tommy.* UK double LP. Track (613 013/4). Released May 23, 1969.

Who, The. *Tommy.* US double LP. Decca (DXSW 7205). Released May 31, 1969.

Who, The. *The Who Sell Out.* UK LP. Track (612 0020) [mono]/(613 002) [stereo]. Released December 16, 1967.

Who, The. *The Who Sell Out.* US LP. Decca (DL 4950) [mono]/(DL 74950) [stereo]. Released January 6, 1968.

Who, The. *The Who Sings My Generation.* US LP. Decca (DL 4664) [mono]/(DL 74664) [stereo]. Released April 1966.

Wilder Evans, Jason, dir. *Record Store Day: The Documentary.* Documentary. Wilder Media Production, 2011.

Zappa, Frank. *We're Only in It for the Money.* US Verve Records (V6-5045). Released March 4, 1968.

Zweig, Alan, dir. *Vinyl.* Documentary. Alan Zweig with production support from the Ontario Arts Council/Canada Council for the Arts, 2000.

Acknowledgments

My primary debt of gratitude goes out to the Society for Critical Exchange and its Winter Theory Institute for providing me with a community of theorists to explore and develop many of the ideas found in this book.

During the course of this project, I have benefited from the insightful conversations and timely suggestions of many individuals, including Christopher Breu, Grant Farred, Barry Faulk, Irving Goh, Robin Truth Goodman, Christian Haines, Peter Hitchcock, Aaron Jaffe, Michael Joyce, Kir Kuiken, Walter Benn Michaels, Paul Allen Miller, Christian Moraru, John Mowitt, Jeffrey T. Nealon, Daniel T. O'Hara, Brian O'Keeffe, Jean Michel Rabaté, Jeffrey A. Sartain, Kyle Schlesinger, Kenneth J. Saltman, Nicole Simek, Raymond B. Stricklin, Henry Sussman, Joe Tabbi, Robert T. Tally, Liane Tanguay, Harold Veeser, and Zahi Zalloua.

Chapter 1 originally appeared in *CR: The New Centennial Review* 18, no. 2 (2018): 107–34. Copyright © 2018 by Michigan State University. A version of chapter 2 was first published as "Adorno on Vinyl" in *Understanding Adorno, Understanding Modernism*, edited by Robin Truth Goodman, Understanding Philosophy, Understanding Modernism, series eds. Paul Ardoin, S. E. Gontarski, and

Laci Mattison (Bloomsbury, 2020). An abbreviated version of chapter 4 appeared as "Who Sells Out Theory?" in *symplokē* 27, nos. 1/2 (2019).

A special note of appreciation goes out to Keri Farnsworth for her editorial support; to Vikki Fitzpatrick for her administrative support, especially in securing materials used for the development of this book; to Paul Vincent Spade of Indiana University for sharing his amazing vinyl collection with me many years ago; and to the late William "Prof" Fielder of Rutgers University for encouraging me in my "formative years," as he would say, to go listen to vinyl in the basement of the university library.

Finally, I would like to thank my "house" band: my sons, Marco (drums) and Orlando (keys), for helping me to see old vinyl through young eyes and, as always, my wife, Nina (bass), for her unfailing encouragement, support, and patience.

Jeffrey R. Di Leo is dean of the School of Arts and Sciences and professor of English and philosophy at the University of Houston-Victoria. He is editor and founder of the critical theory journal *symplokē*, editor and publisher of the *American Book Review*, and executive director of the Society for Critical Exchange. His books include *Morality Matters: Race, Class and Gender in Applied Ethics* (2002); *Affiliations: Identity in Academic Culture* (2003); *On Anthologies: Politics and Pedagogy* (2004); *If Classrooms Matter: Progressive Visions of Educational Environments* (2004, with W. Jacobs); *From Socrates to Cinema: An Introduction to Philosophy* (2007); *Fiction's Present: Situating Contemporary Narrative Innovation* (2008, with R. M. Berry); *Federman's Fictions: Innovation, Theory, and the Holocaust* (2010); *Terror, Theory, and the Humanities* (2012, with U. Mehan); *Academe Degree Zero: Reconsidering the Politics of Higher Education* (2012); *Neoliberalism, Terrorism, Education: Contemporary Dialogues* (2013, with H. Giroux, K. Saltman, and S. McClennen); *Corporate Humanities in Higher Education: Moving beyond the Neoliberal Academy* (2013); *Turning the Page: Book Culture in the Digital Age* (2014); *Criticism after Critique: Aesthetics, Literature, and the Political* (2014); *Dead Theory: Death, Derrida, and the Afterlife of Theory* (2016); *Higher Education under Late Capitalism: Identity, Conduct and the Neoliberal Condition* (2017); *American Literature as World Literature* (2017); *The Debt Age* (2018, with P. Hitchcock and S. McClennen); *The Bloomsbury Handbook of Literary and Cultural Theory* (2019); *The End of American Literature: Essays from the Late Age of Print* (2019); *What's Wrong with Antitheory?* (2020); and *Philosophy as World Literature* (2020).

Index

www.ingramcontent.com/pod-product-compliance
Lightning Source LLC
Chambersburg PA
CBHW060014050426
42448CB00012B/2754